Julia High Performance

Design and develop high performing programs
with Julia

Avik Sengupta

[PACKT] open source*
PUBLISHING
community experience distilled

BIRMINGHAM - MUMBAI

Julia High Performance

First published: April 2016

Production reference: 1220416

Published by Packt Publishing Ltd.
Livery Place
35 Livery Street
Birmingham B3 2PB, UK.

ISBN 978-1-78588-091-9

www.packtpub.com

Credits

Author
Avik Sengupta

Reviewer
QL ZHUO

Commissioning Editor
Priya Singh

Acquisition Editor
Reshma Raman

Content Development Editor
Onkar Wani

Technical Editor
Kunal Chaudhari

Copy Editor
Shruti Iyer

Project Coordinator
Bijal Patel

Proofreader
Safis Editing

Indexer
Rekha Nair

Graphics
Jason Monteiro

Production Coordinator
Manu Joseph

Cover Work
Manu Joseph

About the Author

Avik Sengupta has worked on risk and trading systems in investment banking for many years, mostly using Java interspersed with snippets of the exotic R and K languages. This experience left him wondering whether there were better things out there. Avik's quest came to a happy conclusion with the appearance of Julia in 2012. He has been happily coding in Julia and contributing to it ever since.

This book was only possible because four intrepid computer scientists decided they wanted a better language six years ago. So, I would like to thank Alan, Jeff, Stefan, and Viral for giving Julia to the world. The world of scientific computing has changed drastically as a result.

Working in Julia over the last three years has been one of the most enjoyable experiences in my professional career. A large part of this joy is due to the people who inhabit this community. It is a collection of smart and engaged scientists and developers who have taught me far more than programming languages. A big "thank you" goes to the entire Julia community, which is responsible for all the buzz that Julia has received.

Many thanks are due to the reviewers who generously provided their time to improve this book. While all the deficiencies remain my own, this is now a much better product thanks to their efforts.

Writing a book turned out to need many more late nights than I would have thought necessary. So, I would like to give a big shout-out to Vaishali and Ahan for keeping me sane and well-fed during this process.

About the Reviewer

QL ZHUO (also known as KDr2 online) is an open source developer from China who has about 10 years experience with Linux, C, C++, Java, Python, and Perl development. He loves participating in and contributing to the open source community, which, of course, includes the Julia community. QL maintains a personal website at `http://kdr2.com`, and you can find out more about him there.

www.PacktPub.com

Support files, eBooks, discount offers, and more

For support files and downloads related to your book, please visit www.PacktPub.com.

Did you know that Packt offers eBook versions of every book published, with PDF and ePub files available? You can upgrade to the eBook version at www.PacktPub.com and as a print book customer, you are entitled to a discount on the eBook copy. Get in touch with us at service@packtpub.com for more details.

At www.PacktPub.com, you can also read a collection of free technical articles, sign up for a range of free newsletters and receive exclusive discounts and offers on Packt books and eBooks.

https://www2.packtpub.com/books/subscription/packtlib

Do you need instant solutions to your IT questions? PacktLib is Packt's online digital book library. Here, you can search, access, and read Packt's entire library of books.

Why subscribe?

- Fully searchable across every book published by Packt
- Copy and paste, print, and bookmark content
- On demand and accessible via a web browser

Table of Contents

Preface

When I first learned about Julia in early 2012, it was clear to me that this is a language that I've wanted for many years. The use of multiple dispatch made it very easy to express mathematical concepts, while the speed of the language made it feasible to express them in the Julia. I came for the elegance and stayed for the performance. On the other hand, some users come to Julia for the performance and stay for the elegance. Either way, in order to fully appreciate the power and beauty of the language, it needs to live up to its promise of high performance.

I hope this book will help Julia programmers at all levels to learn the design techniques and paradigms that produce fast Julia code. One of the nice things about Julia is that its performance characteristics are simple and easy to reason out. I hope this book will provide you with a framework to think about and analyze the performance of your own code.

What this book covers

Chapter 1, Julia is Fast, discusses some of the design underpinning the language and its focus on high performance.

Chapter 2, Analyzing Julia Performance, provides the tools and techniques you can use to measure and analyze the performance of your own programs.

Chapter 3, Types in Julia, describes the type system and discusses why writing type-stable code is crucial to high performance.

Chapter 4, Functions and Macros – Structuring Julia Code for High Performance, discusses techniques to use dispatch and code generation to structure high-performance programs.

Chapter 5, Fast Numbers, discusses the basic numeric types and why they are fast.

Chapter 6, Fast Arrays, describes ways to use multidimensional arrays in the fastest possible way.

Chapter 7, Beyond the Single Processor, provides an introduction to Julia's distributed computing facilities.

What you need for this book

If you are reading this book, we assume you have installed Julia and written a few simple Julia programs and that you are familiar with Julia REPL. The basic Julia installation, available from http://julialang.org/downloads, is the only prerequisite for this book. We will demonstrate most of the techniques in the book using REPL, and we encourage your to follow along. Paste the commands on to REPL and inspect the output yourself.

Who this book is for

This book is for beginner- and intermediate-level Julia developers who are interested in high-performance technical computing. We expect you to have a basic understanding of Julia's syntax and have written a few small Julia programs prior to reading this book.

Conventions

In this book, you will find a number of text styles that distinguish between different kinds of information. Here are some examples of these styles and an explanation of their meaning.

Code words in text, database table names, folder names, filenames, file extensions, pathnames, dummy URLs, user input, and Twitter handles are shown as follows: "abstract types are defined using the abstract keyword."

A block of code is set as follows:

```
function bar(a, b)
    x::Int64 = 0
    y = a+b+x
    return y
end
```

Any command-line input or output is written as follows:

```
julia> @benchmark serial_add()
================ Benchmark Results ========================
Time per evaluation: 6.95 ms [6.59 ms, 7.31 ms]
Proportion of time in GC: 0.00% [0.00%, 0.00%]
Memory allocated: 0.00 bytes
Number of allocations: 0 allocations
Number of samples: 100
Number of evaluations: 100
Time spent benchmarking: 0.86 s
```

New terms and **important words** are shown in bold.

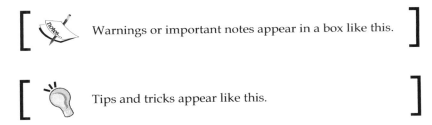

> Warnings or important notes appear in a box like this.

> Tips and tricks appear like this.

Reader feedback

Feedback from our readers is always welcome. Let us know what you think about this book—what you liked or disliked. Reader feedback is important for us as it helps us develop titles that you will really get the most out of.

To send us general feedback, simply e-mail feedback@packtpub.com, and mention the book's title in the subject of your message.

If there is a topic that you have expertise in and you are interested in either writing or contributing to a book, see our author guide at www.packtpub.com/authors.

Customer support

Now that you are the proud owner of a Packt book, we have a number of things to help you to get the most from your purchase.

Downloading the example code

You can download the example code files for this book from your account at
http://www.packtpub.com. If you purchased this book elsewhere, you can visit
http://www.packtpub.com/support and register to have the files e-mailed directly
to you.

You can download the code files by following these steps:

1. Log in or register to our website using your e-mail address and password.
2. Hover the mouse pointer on the **SUPPORT** tab at the top.
3. Click on **Code Downloads & Errata**.
4. Enter the name of the book in the **Search** box.
5. Select the book for which you're looking to download the code files.
6. Choose from the drop-down menu where you purchased this book from.
7. Click on **Code Download**.

You can also download the code files by clicking on the **Code Files** button on
the book's webpage at the Packt Publishing website. This page can be accessed
by entering the book's name in the **Search** box. Please note that you need to be
logged in to your Packt account.

Once the file is downloaded, please make sure that you unzip or extract the folder
using the latest version of:

- WinRAR / 7-Zip for Windows
- Zipeg / iZip / UnRarX for Mac
- 7-Zip / PeaZip for Linux

Downloading the color images of this book

We also provide you with a PDF file that has color images of the screenshots/diagrams
used in this book. The color images will help you better understand the changes in
the output. You can download this file from https://www.packtpub.com/sites/
default/files/downloads/JuliaHighPerformance_ColorImages.pdf.

Errata

Although we have taken every care to ensure the accuracy of our content, mistakes do happen. If you find a mistake in one of our books—maybe a mistake in the text or the code—we would be grateful if you could report this to us. By doing so, you can save other readers from frustration and help us improve subsequent versions of this book. If you find any errata, please report them by visiting http://www.packtpub. com/submit-errata, selecting your book, clicking on the **Errata Submission Form** link, and entering the details of your errata. Once your errata are verified, your submission will be accepted and the errata will be uploaded to our website or added to any list of existing errata under the Errata section of that title.

To view the previously submitted errata, go to https://www.packtpub.com/books/ content/support and enter the name of the book in the search field. The required information will appear under the **Errata** section.

Piracy

Piracy of copyrighted material on the Internet is an ongoing problem across all media. At Packt, we take the protection of our copyright and licenses very seriously. If you come across any illegal copies of our works in any form on the Internet, please provide us with the location address or website name immediately so that we can pursue a remedy.

Please contact us at copyright@packtpub.com with a link to the suspected pirated material.

We appreciate your help in protecting our authors and our ability to bring you valuable content.

Questions

If you have a problem with any aspect of this book, you can contact us at questions@packtpub.com, and we will do our best to address the problem.

1
Julia is Fast

In many ways, the history of programming languages has often been driven by, and certainly intertwined, with the needs of numerical and scientific computing. The first high-level programming language, Fortran, was created with scientific computing in mind, and continues to be important in the field even to this day. In recent years, the rise of data science as a specialty has brought additional focus to scientific computing, particularly for statistical uses. In this area, somewhat counterintuitively, both specialized languages such as R and general-purpose languages such as Python are in widespread use. The rise of Hadoop and Spark has spread the use of Java and Scala respectively among this community. In the midst of all this, Matlab has had a strong niche within engineering and communities, while Mathematica remains unparalleled for symbolic operations.

A new language for scientific computing therefore has a very high barrier to overcome. It's been only a few short years since the Julia language was introduced into the world. In this time, it's innovative features, which make it a dynamic language, based on multiple dispatch as its defining paradigm, has created growing niche within the numerical computing world. However, it's the claim of high performance that excited its early adopters the most.

This, then, is a book that celebrates writing high-performance programs. With Julia, this is not only possible, but also reasonably straightforward, within a low-overhead, dynamic language.

As a reader of this book, you have likely already written your first few Julia programs. We will assume that you have successfully installed Julia, and have a working programming environment available. We expect you are familiar with very basic Julia syntax, but we will discuss and review many of those concepts throughout the book as we introduce them.

- Julia – fast and dynamic
- Designed for speed
- How fast can Julia be?

Julia – fast and dynamic

It is a widely believed myth in programming language communities that high-performance languages and dynamic languages are completely disjoint sets. The perceived wisdom is that, if you want programmer productivity, you should use a dynamic language, such as Ruby, Python or R. On the other hand, if you want fast code execution, you should use a statically typed language such as C or Java.

There are always exceptions to this rule. However, for most mainstream programmers, this is a strongly held belief.

This usually manifests itself in what is known as the "two language" problem. This is something that is especially prominent in scientific computing. This is the situation where the performance-critical inner kernel is written in C, but is then wrapped and used from a dynamic, higher-level language. Code written in traditional, scientific computing environments such as R, Matlab or NumPy follows this paradigm.

Code written in this fashion is not without its drawbacks however. Even though it looks like this gets you the best of both worlds — fast computation, while allowing the programmer to use a high-level language — this is a path full of hidden dangers. For one, someone will have to write the low-level kernel. So, you need two different skillsets. If you are lucky to find the low level code in C for your project, you are fine. However, if you are doing anything new or original, or even slightly different from the norm, you will find yourself writing both C and a high-level language. This severely limits the number of contributors that your projects or research will get: to be really productive, they have to be familiar with two languages.

Secondly, when running code routinely written in two languages, there can be severe and unforeseen performance pitfalls. When you can drop down to C code quickly, everything is fine. However, if, for whatever reason, your code cannot call into a C routine, you'll find your program taking hundreds or even thousands of times more longer than you expected.

Julia is the first modern language to make a reasonable effort to solve the "two language" problem. It is a high-level, dynamic, language with powerful features that make for a very productive programmer. At the same time, code written in Julia usually runs very fast, almost as fast as code written in statically typed languages.

The rest of this chapter describes some of the underlying design decisions that make Julia such a fast language. We also see some evidence of the performance claims for Julia.

The rest of the book shows you how to write your Julia programs in a way that optimizes its time and memory usage to the maximum. We will discuss how to measure and reason performance in Julia, and how to avoid potential performance pitfalls.

For all the content in this book, we will illustrate our point individually with small and simple programs. We hope that this will enable you grasp the crux of the issue, without getting distracted by unnecessary elements of a larger program. We expect that this methodology will therefore provide you with an instinctive intuition about Julia's performance profile.

Julia has a refreshingly simple performance model – and thus writing fast Julia code is a matter of understanding a few key elements of computer architecture, and how the Julia compiler interacts with it. We hope that, by the end of this book, your instincts are well developed to design and write your own Julia code with the fastest possible performance.

Versions of Julia

Julia is a fast moving project, with an open development process. All the code and examples in this book are targeted at version 0.4 of the language, which is the currently released version at the time of publication. Check Packt's website for changes and errata for future versions of Julia.

Designed for speed

When the creators of Julia launched the language into the world, they said the following in a blog post entitled *Why We Created Julia*, which was published in early 2012:

> *"We want a language that's open source, with a liberal license. We want the speed of C with the dynamism of Ruby. We want a language that's homoiconic, with true macros like Lisp, but with obvious, familiar mathematical notation like Matlab. We want something as usable for general programming as Python, as easy for statistics as R, as natural for string processing as Perl, as powerful for linear algebra as Matlab, as good at gluing programs together as the shell. Something that is dirt simple to learn, yet keeps the most serious hackers happy. We want it interactive and we want it compiled.*
>
> *(Did we mention it should be as fast as C?)"*

High performance, indeed nearly C-level performance, has therefore been one of the founding principles of the language. It's built from the ground up to enable a fast execution of code.

In addition to being a core design principle, it has also been a necessity from the early stages of its development. A very large part of Julia's standard library, including very basic low-level operations, is written in Julia itself. For example, the + operation to add two integers is defined in Julia itself. (Refer to: https://github.com/JuliaLang/julia/blob/1986c5024db36b4c921130351597f5b4f9f81691/base/int.jl#L8). Similarly, the basic for loop uses the standard iteration mechanism available to all user-defined types. This means that the implementation had to be very fast from the very beginning to create a usable language. The creators of Julia did not have the luxury of escaping to C for even the core elements of the library.

We will note throughout the book many design decisions that have been made with an eye to high performance. But there are three main elements that create the basis for Julia's speed.

JIT and LLVM

Julia is a **Just In Time (JIT)** compiled language, rather than an interpreted one. This allows Julia to be dynamic, without having the overhead of interpretation. This compilation infrastructure is build on top of **Low Level Virtual Machine (LLVM)** (http://llvm.org).

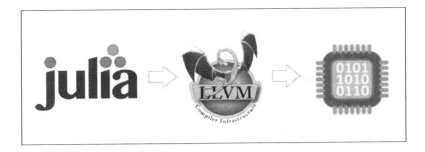

The LLVM compiler without infrastructure project originated at University of Illinois. It now has contributions from a very large number of corporate as well as independent developers. As a result of all this work, it is now a very high-quality, yet modular, system for many different compilation and code generation activities.

Julia uses LLVM for its JIT compilation needs. The Julia runtime generates LLVM **Intermediate Representation (IR)** and hands it over to LLVM's JIT compiler, which in turn generates machine code that is executed on the CPU. As a result, sophisticated compilation techniques that are built into LLVM are ready and available to Julia, from the simple (such as *Loop Unrolling* or *Loop Deletion*) to state-of-the-art (such as *SIMD Vectorization*) ones. These compiler optimizations form a very large body of work, and in this sense, the existence is of LLVM is very much a pre-requisite to the existence of Julia. It would have been an almost impossible task for a small team of developers to build this infrastructure from scratch.

Just-In-Time compilation

Just-in-Time compilation is a technique in which the code in a high-level language is converted to machine code for execution on the CPU at runtime. This is in contrast to interpreted languages, whose runtime executes the source language directly. This usually has a significantly higher overhead. On the other hand, **Ahead of Time (AOT)** compilation refers to the technique of converting source language into machine code as a separate step prior to running the code. In this case, the converted machine code can usually be saved to disk as an executable file.

Types

We will have much more to say about types in Julia throughout this book. At this stage, suffice it to say that Julia's concept of types is a key ingredient in its performance.

The Julia compiler tries to infer the type of all data used in a program, and compiles different versions of functions specialized to particular types of its arguments. To take a simple example, consider the sqrt function. This function can be called with integer or floating-point arguments. Julia will compile two versions of the code, one for integer arguments, and one for floating point arguments. This means that, at runtime, fast, straight-line code without any type checks will be executed on the CPU.

The ability of the compiler to reason about types is due to the combination of a sophisticated dataflow-based algorithm, and careful language design that allows this information to be inferred from most programs before execution begins. Put in another way, the language is designed to make it easy to statically analyze.

If there is a single reason for Julia is being such a high-performance language, this is it. This is why Julia is able to run at C-like speeds while still being a dynamic language. *Type inference* and *code specialization* are as close to a secret sauce as Julia gets. It is notable that, outside this type inference mechanism, the Julia compiler is quite simple. It does not include many advanced Just in Time optimizations that Java and JavaScript compilers are known to use. When the compiler has enough information about the types within the code, it can generate optimized, straight-line, code without many of these advanced techniques.

It is useful to note here that unlike some other optionally typed dynamic languages, simply adding type annotations to your code does not usually make Julia go any faster. Type inference means that the compiler is, in most cases, able to figure out the types of variables when necessary. Hence you can usually write high-level code without fighting with the compiler about types, and still achieve superior performance.

How fast can Julia be?

The best evidence of Julia's performance claims is when you write your own code. However, we can provide an indication of how fast Julia can be by comparing a similar algorithm over multiple languages.

As an example, let's consider a very simple routine to calculate the power sum for a series, as follows:

$$\sum_{n=1}^{1000} \frac{1}{n^2}$$

The following code runs this computation in Julia 500 times:

```
function pisum()
    sum = 0.0
    for j = 1:500
        sum = 0.0
        for k = 1:10000
            sum += 1.0/(k*k)
        end
    end
    sum
end
```

You will notice that this code contains no type annotations. It should look quite familiar to any modern dynamic language. The same algorithm implemented in C would look something similar to this:

```
double pisum() {
    double sum = 0.0;
    for (int j=0; j<500; ++j) {
        sum = 0.0;
        for (int k=1; k<=10000; ++k) {
            sum += 1.0/(k*k);
        }
    }
    return sum;
}
```

Downloading the example code

You can download the example code files for this book from your account at http://www.packtpub.com. If you purchased this book elsewhere, you can visit http://www.packtpub.com/support and register to have the files e-mailed directly to you.

You can download the code files by following these steps:

- Log in or register to our website using your e-mail address and password
- Let the mouse pointer hover on the **SUPPORT** tab at the top
- Click on **Code Downloads & Errata**
- Enter the name of the book in the **Search** box
- Select the book for which you're looking to download the code files
- Choose from the drop-down menu where you purchased this book from
- Click on **Code Download**

You can also download the code files by clicking on the **Code Files** button on the book's webpage at the Packt Publishing website. This page can be accessed by entering the book's name in the **Search** box. Please note that you need to be logged in to your Packt account.

Once the file is downloaded, please make sure that you unzip or extract the folder using the latest version of:

- WinRAR/7-Zip for Windows
- Zipeg/iZip/UnRarX for Mac
- 7-Zip/PeaZip for Linux

By timing this code, and its re-implementation in many other languages (all of which are available at https://github.com/JuliaLang/julia/tree/master/test/perf/micro), we can note that Julia's performance claims are certainly borne out in this limited test. Julia can perform at a level similar to C and other statically typed and compiled languages.

This is of course a micro benchmark, and should therefore not be extrapolated too much. However, I hope you will agree that it is possible to achieve excellent performance in Julia. The rest of the book will attempt to show how you can achieve performance close to this standard in your code.

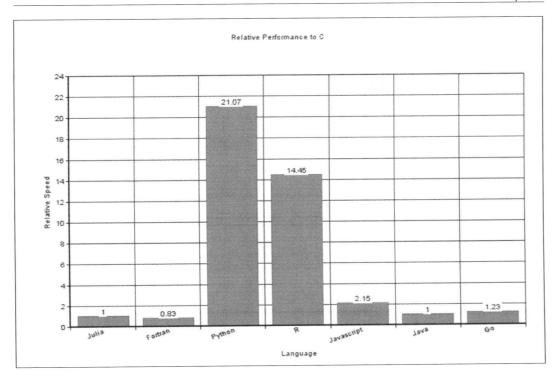

Summary

In this chapter, you noted that Julia is a language that is built from the ground up for high performance. Its design and implementation have always been focused on providing the highest possible performance on the modern CPU.

The rest of the book will show you how to use the power of Julia to the maximum, to write the fastest possible code in this language. In the next chapter, we will discuss how to measure the speed of Julia code, and identify performance bottlenecks. You will learn some of the tools that are built into Julia for this purpose.

2
Analyzing Julia Performance

Before we can try and optimize any Julia code we have written, we first need to understand its performance characteristics. Is the code fast enough for our needs? If not, how much slower is it from what it needs to be? And finally, can we understand where the bottlenecks are, so that we can prioritize where to focus our optimization effort? This chapter will show us the tools available in Julia to answer these questions and more. In later chapters, we will take a look at how to use this information to optimize our code.

In this chapter we will cover the following topics:

- Timing Julia functions
- Accurate benchmarking
- Profiling Julia functions
- Tracking detailed memory allocation

Timing Julia code

The first step to understanding anything is to measure it. The same goes for writing high-performance Julia code; we need to measure the performance of the code as the first step to achieving this. Fortunately Julia makes this extremely easy for us. There are simple ways to measure the time taken by any Julia code built into the Julia runtime. Moreover, if you want to perform statistically accurate benchmarking, there are high-quality packages available.

Tic and Toc

The simplest way to measure time in Julia is using the `tic()` and `toc()` functions. Place these functions respectively before and after any piece of Julia code, and we will note the time taken by this code on the console. Run the following code:

```
julia> tic(); sqrt(rand(1000)); toc();
elapsed time: 0.000137693 seconds
```

In the preceding code, we measured the time taken to generate 1,000 random numbers, and to compute its square root. Technically, all the `toc()` function does is print the `elapsed time` value since the last invocation of `tic()`. The time printed in this case (and other cases) is the actual `elapsed time` value, not the time spent by the CPU on the process. In other words, this is the wall-clock time. In particular, this time can be affected by any other CPU's intensive processes running on the machine at the same time.

Using these functions might be convenient when running a script, but it is not convenient during interactive development on Julia's **Read Eval Print Load** (**REPL**) console. Therefore, the most common way to measure the elapsed time of Julia code is to use the `@time` macro, which we will discuss next.

The @time macro

Whenever you care about the performance of your code (which you should do all the time), the `@time` macro will end up being one of your most used commands on the Julia prompt. Built into the runtime, this macro wraps the provided expression to calculate and print the elapsed time while running it. It also measures and outputs the amount of memory allocated while running this code as follows:

```
julia> @time sqrt(rand(1000));
  0.000023 seconds (8 allocations: 15.969 KB)
```

Any kind of Julia expression can be wrapped by the `@time` macro. Usually, it is a function call as before, but it could be any other valid expression as follows:

```
julia> s=0
0

julia> @time for i=1:1000
           s=s+sqrt(i)
       end
  0.001270 seconds (2.40 k allocations: 54.058 KB)
```

Timing measurements and JIT compiling

Recall that Julia is a JIT compiled language. The Julia compiler and runtime compiles any Julia code into machine code the first time it sees it. This means that, if you measure the execution time of any Julia expression that executes for the first time, you will end up measuring the time (and memory use) required to compile this code. So, whenever you time any piece of Julia code, it is crucial to run it at least once, prior to measuring the execution time. Always measure the second or later invocation.

The @timev macro

An enhanced version of the @time macro is also available: the @timev macro. This macro operates in a very similar manner to @time, but measures some additional memory statistics, and provides elapsed time measurements with nanosecond precision. Take a look at the following code:

```
julia> @timev sqrt(rand(1000));
  0.000012 seconds (8 allocations: 15.969 KB)
elapsed time (ns): 11551
bytes allocated:    16352
pool allocs:        6
non-pool GC allocs:2
```

Both the @time and @timev macros return the value of the expression whose performance they measured. Hence, these can be added without side-effects to almost any location within the Julia code.

The Julia profiler

The Julia runtime includes a built-in profiler that can be used to measure which lines of code contribute the most to the total execution time of a codebase. It can therefore be used to identify bottlenecks in code, which can in turn be used to prioritize optimization efforts.

This built-in system is what is known as a *sampling profiler*. Its work is to inspect the call stack of the running system every few milliseconds (by default, 1 millisecond on UNIX and 10 milliseconds on Windows), and identify each line of code that contributes to this call stack. The idea is that the lines of code that are executed most often are found more often on the call stack. Hence, over many such samples, the count of how often each line of code is encountered will be a measure of how often this code runs.

The primary advantage of a sampling profiler is that it can run without modifying the source program, and thus has a very minimal overhead. The program runs at almost full speed when being profiled. The downside of the profiler is that the data is statistical in nature, and may not reflect exactly how the program performed. However, when sampled over a reasonable period of time (say a few hundred milliseconds at least), the results are accurate enough to provide a good understanding of how the program performs, and what its bottlenecks are.

Using the profiler

The profiler code lives within the profile module within Julia. So the first step in using the profiler is to import its namespace into the current session. You can do this via the following code.

```
julia> using Base.Profile
```

This makes the @profile macro available to measure and store the performance profile of the expression supplied to it.

Do not profile the JIT

As with measuring the time of execution, remember to run your code at least once before attempting to profile it. Otherwise, you will end up profiling the Julia JIT compiler, rather than your code.

To see how the profiler works, let's start with a test function that creates 1,000 sets of 10,000 random numbers, and then computes the standard deviation of each set. Run the following:

```
function testfunc()
    x = rand(10000, 1000)
    y = std(x, 1)
    return y
end
```

After calling the function once to ensure that all the code is compiled, we can run the profiler over this code. as follows:

```
julia> @profile testfunc()
```

This will execute the expression while collecting profile information. The expression will return as usual, and the collected profile information will be stored in memory.

```
julia> Profile.print()
34 REPL.jl; anonymous; line: 93
```

```
34 REPL.jl; eval_user_input; line: 63
 34 profile.jl; anonymous; line: 16
  21 random.jl; rand!; line: 347
   21 dSFMT.jl; dsfmt_fill_array_close_open!; line: 76
  12 statistics.jl; var; line: 169
   1 reducedim.jl; reduced_dims; line: 19
   6 statistics.jl; mean; line: 31
    6 reducedim.jl; sum!; line: 258
     6 reducedim.jl; _mapreducedim!; line: 197
      4 reduce.jl; mapreduce_pairwise_impl; line: 111
       2 reduce.jl; mapreduce_pairwise_impl; line: 111
        . . .
       2 reduce.jl; mapreduce_pairwise_impl; line: 112
        . . .
       2 reduce.jl; mapreduce_pairwise_impl; line: 112
       2 reduce.jl; mapreduce_pairwise_impl; line: 111
        . . .
   5 statistics.jl; varm!; line: 152
    5 statistics.jl; centralize_sumabs2!; line: 117
     4 reduce.jl; mapreduce_pairwise_impl; line: 111
      4 reduce.jl; mapreduce_pairwise_impl; line: 112
       2 reduce.jl; mapreduce_pairwise_impl; line: 111
        2 reduce.jl; mapreduce_pairwise_impl; line: 111
         2 reduce.jl; mapreduce_pairwise_impl; line: 108
          2 simdloop.jl; mapreduce_seq_impl; line: 67
        2 reduce.jl; mapreduce_pairwise_impl; line: 112
         . . .
```

As you can note, the output from the profiler is a hierarchical list of code locations, representing the call stack for the program. The number against each line counts the number of times this line was sampled by the profiler. Therefore, the higher the number, the greater the contribution of that line to the total runtime of the program. It indicates the time spent on the line, and all its *callees*.

What does this output tell us? Well, among other things, it shows that the creation of the random arrays took most of the execution time, about two-thirds. For the remainder of the calculation of the standard deviation, the time was evenly split between the computation of the mean and variance.

There are a few profiler options that are sometimes useful, although the defaults are a good choice for most use cases. Primary among them is the *sampling interval*. This can be provided as keyword arguments to the `Profile.init()` method. The default delay is 1 millisecond on Linux, and should be increased for very long-running programs through the following line of code:

```
julia> Profile.init(delay=.01)
```

The delay may be reduced as well, but the overhead of profiling can increase significantly if it is lowered too much.

Finally, you may have realized that the profiler stores its samples in memory to be viewed later. In order to profile a different program during an existing Julia session, it may be necessary to clear the stored profile from memory. The `Profile.clear()` function does this, and must therefore be run between any two invocations of `@profile` within the same Julia process.

ProfileView

The textual display of the profiler output shown before is useful and elucidating in many cases, but can get confusing if read for long, or deeply nested call graphs. In this case, or in general if you would prefer a graphical output, the `ProfileView` package provides such an output. However, this is not built in to the base of Julia, and must be installed as an external package

```
Pkg.add("ProfileView")
```

This will install the `ProfileView` package and its dependencies (which include the Tk graphical environment). Once installed, its usage is very simple. Simply call the `ProfileView.view()` function instead of `Profile.print()` after the profile samples have been collected using `@profile`. A user interface window will pop up, with the profile displayed as a *flame graph*, looking similar to the following screenshot. Move your cursor over the blocks to note a hover containing the details of the call location:

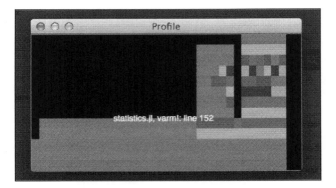

This view provides the same information as the tree view seen earlier, but may be easier to navigate and understand, particularly for larger programs. In this chart, elapsed time goes from left to right, while the call stack goes from bottom to top. The width of the bar therefore shows the time spent by the program in a particular call location and its callees. The bars stacked on top of one another show a call from one to the other.

Analyzing memory allocation

The amount of memory used by a program is sometimes as important to track as the amount of time taken to run it. This is not only because memory is a limited resource that can be in short supply, but also because excessive allocation can easily lead to excessive execution time. The time taken to allocate and de-allocate memory and run the garbage collection can become quite significant when a program uses large amounts of memory.

The `@time` macro seen in the previous sections provides information about memory allocation for the expression or function being timed. In some cases however it may be difficult to predict where exactly in the code the memory allocation occurs. For these situations, Julia's track allocation functionality is just what is needed.

Using the memory allocation tracker

To get Julia to track memory allocation, start the `julia` process with the `-track-allocation=user` option as follows:

```
julia> track -allocation=user
```

This will start a normal Julia session in which you can run your code as usual. However, in the background, Julia will track all the memory used, which will be written to `.mem` files when Julia exits. There will be a new `.mem` file for each `.jl` file that is loaded and executed. These files will contain the Julia code from their corresponding source files, with each line annotated with the total amount of memory that was allocated as a result of executing this line.

As we discussed before, when running Julia code, the compiler will compile user code at runtime. Once again, we do not want to measure the memory allocation due to the compiler. To achieve this, first run the code under measurement once, after starting the Julia process. Then run the `Profile.clear_malloc_data()` function to restart the allocation measurement counters. Finally, run the code under measurement once again, and then exit the process. This way, we will get the most accurate memory measurements.

Statistically accurate benchmarking

The tools described in this chapter, particularly the @time macro, are useful to identify and investigate bottlenecks in our program. However, they are not very accurate for a fine-grained analysis of fast programs. If you want to, for example, compare two functions that take a few milliseconds to run, the amount of error and variability in the measurement will easily swamp the running time of this function.

Using Benchmarks.jl

The solution then is to use the Benchmarks.jl package for statistically accurate benchmarking. This package is not yet published in the official repository, but is stable and high-quality nevertheless. It can be installed with Pkg.clone("https://github.com/johnmyleswhite/Benchmarks.jl.git") and the subsequent usage is simple. Instead of using @time, as before, simply use @benchmark. Unlike @time however, this macro can only be used in front of function calls, rather than any expression. It will evaluate the parameters of the function separately, and then call the function multiple times to build up a sample of execution times.

The output will show the mean time taken to run the code, but with statistically accurate upper and lower bounds. These statistics are computed using an ordinary least squares fit of the measured execution time to estimate the expected distribution. Take a look at the following:

```
julia> using Benchmarks

julia> @benchmark sqrt(rand(1000))

================ Benchmark Results ========================
      Time per evaluation: 9.48 µs [9.26 µs, 9.69 µs]
 Proportion of time in GC: 5.43% [4.22%, 6.65%]
        Memory allocated: 15.81 kb
    Number of allocations: 4 allocations
        Number of samples: 6601
    Number of evaluations: 1080001
        R² of OLS model: 0.913
 Time spent benchmarking: 10.28 s
```

Summary

In this chapter, we discussed how to use the available tools to measure the performance of Julia code. You learned to measure the time and memory resources used by code, and understood the hotspots for any program.

In subsequent chapters, you will learn how to fix the issues that we identified using these tools, and make our Julia programs perform at their fastest.

3
Types in Julia

Julia is a dynamically typed language in which, unlike languages such as Java or C, the programmer does not need to specify the fixed type of every variable in the program. Yet, somewhat counterintuitively, Julia achieves its impressive performance characteristics by inferring and using type information for all the data in the program. In this chapter, we will start with a brief look at the type system in the language and then explain how to use this type system to write high-performance code.

- The Julia type system
- Type-stability
- Types at storage locations

The Julia type system

Types in Julia are essentially tag-on values that restrict the range of potential values that can possibly be stored at this location. Being a dynamic language, these tags are relevant only to runtime values. Types are not enforced at compile time (except in rare cases); rather, they are checked at runtime. However, type information is used at compile time to generate specialized methods and different kinds of function argument.

Using types

In most dynamic languages, types are usually implicit in how values are created. Julia can, and usually is, written in this way — with no explicit type annotations. However, additionally in Julia, you can specify that variables or function parameters should be restricted to specific types using the :: symbol. Here's an example:

```
foo(x::Integer) = "an integer"      #Declare type of function argument
foo(x::ASCIIString) = "a string"
```

```
function bar(a, b)
    x::Int64 = 0          #Declare type of local variable
    y = a+b               #Type of variable will be inferred
    return y
end


julia> foo(1)            #Dispatch on type of argument
"an integer"


julia> foo("1")          #Dispatch on type of argument
"a string"


julia> foo(1.5)          #Dispatch fails
ERROR: `foo` has no method matching foo(::Float64)
```

A note on terminology

In Julia, an abstract operation represented by a name is called a function, while the individual implementations for specific types are called methods. Thus, in the preceding code, we can talk of the foo function and the foo methods for Integer and ASCIIString.

Multiple dispatch

If there were one unifying strand through the design of the Julia language, it would be *multiple dispatch*. Simply put, dispatch is the process of selecting a function to be executed at runtime. Multiple dispatch, then, is the method of determining the function to be called based on the types of all the parameters of the function. Thus, one of the most important uses of types in Julia programs is to arrange the appropriate method dispatch by specifying the types of function arguments.

Note that this is different from the concept of method overloading. Dispatch is a runtime process, while method overloading is a compile-time concept. In most traditional object-oriented languages, dispatch at runtime occurs only on the runtime type of the *receiver* of the method (for example, the object before the dot)—hence the term "single dispatch."

Julia programs, therefore, usually contain many small function definitions for different types of arguments. It is good practice, however, to constrain argument types to the widest level possible. Use tight constraints only when you know that the method will fail on other types. Otherwise, write your method to accept unconstrained types and depend on the runtime to dispatch nested calls to the correct methods.

As an example, consider the following function to compute the sum of the square of two numbers:

```
sumsqr(x, y) = x^2 + y^2
```

In this code, we do not specify any type constraints for the x and y arguments of our sumsqr function. The base library will contain different + and ^ methods for integers and floats, and the runtime will dispatch to the correct method based on the types of the arguments. Take a look at the output:

```
julia> sumsqr(1, 2)
5

julia> sumsqr(1.5, 2.5)
8.5

julia> sumsqr(1 + 2im , 2 + 3im)
-8 + 16im
```

Abstract types

Types in Julia can be concrete or abstract. Abstract types cannot have any instantiated values. In other words, they can only be the nodes of the type hierarchy, not its leaves. They represent sets of related types. For example, Julia contains integer types for 32-bit and 64-bit integers — Int32 and Int64, respectively. Both these types therefore inherit from the Integer abstract type.

Abstract types are defined using the abstract keyword. The inheritance relationship between types is denoted using the <: symbol followed by the name of the parent (or super) type. As an example, shown here are the abstract types defined as the basis of Julia's number types:

```
abstract Number
abstract Real        <: Number
abstract FloatingPoint <: Real
abstract Integer     <: Real
abstract Signed      <: Integer
abstract Unsigned    <: Integer
```

You will notice that the Number type is declared without any explicit super type. Hence, as discussed in the next section, it is the direct subtype of Any.

Concrete types, on the other hand, are the types that can be instantiated to values. Thus, every value in Julia is of one concrete type. One of the most important points to note about concrete types is that they cannot have any subtypes. Only abstract types can be subtyped. In the language of type theory, all concrete types are declared final in Julia.

Julia's type hierarchy

All types in Julia live within a type hierarchy. This hierarchy is rooted at the top by the Any type. All Julia types without exception live within this hierarchy. In particular, unlike languages such as Java, there is no distinction between so-called primitive types and reference types. While there may be differences in how the numbers are represented internally compared to user-defined types, as far as the type system is concerned they form a unified hierarchy.

When a type declaration is omitted for a variable or parameter (as in many of the examples in the previous chapter), it can contain values of any type. This is denoted by the special Any type. The Any type can therefore be seen as being at the top of Julia's type hierarchy. All other Julia types are subtypes of this type. Visualizing the type hierarchy of some of the numeric types described in the previous chapter is instructive, as follows:

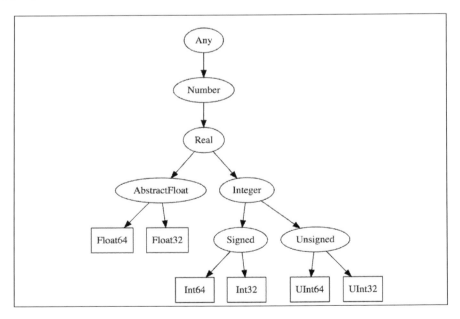

At the other end of the spectrum resides the None type. This type lives at the bottom of the type hierarchy. All types are super types of None, and there can be no actual instances of this type.

Another special type is the Void type. This type has a single instance defined named nothing. This is typically used to denote the absence of a value. For example, methods that don't return any other value (for instance, a return type of void in some languages), return nothing.

Composite and immutable types

Composite types in Julia are collections of named fields. They are equivalent to a struct in C and can be thought of as roughly equivalent to a class without behavior in object-oriented languages. They are defined with the type keyword and contain the names and types of the fields within them. Take a look at the following code:

```
type Pixel
    x::Int64
    y::Int64
    color::Int64
end
```

```
julia> p = Pixel(5,5, 100)
Pixel(5,5,100)

julia> p.x = 10;

julia> p.x
10
```

By default, the fields of a composite type can be changed at any time. In cases where this is undesirable, an immutable type can be declared using the immutable keyword. In this case, field values can be set only while constructing an instance of the type. Once created, field values cannot change. Take a look at the following code:

```
immutable IPixel
    x::Int64
    y::Int64
    color::Int64
end
```

```
julia> p = IPixel(5,5, 100)
IPixel(5,5,100)

julia> p.x=10
ERROR: type IPixel is immutable
```

Type parameters

Type parameters are one of the most useful and powerful features of Julia's type system. This is the ability to use parameters when defining types (or functions), thereby defining a whole set of types, one for each value of the parameter. This is analogous to generic or template programming in other languages.

Type parameters are declared within curly braces. For the preceding `Pixel` type, if we wanted to store `color` as an integer, a hexadecimal string, or as an RGB type, we could write it as follows. In this case, `Pixel` itself becomes an abstract type, and `Pixel{Int64}` or `Pixel{ASCIIString}` are the concrete types:

```
type Pixel{T}
    x::Int64
    y::Int64
    color::T
end
```

Parameters of a type are usually other types. This will be familiar if you have used template classes in C++ or Java generics. In Julia, however, type parameters are not restricted to be other types. They can be values though they are restricted to a set of constant, immutable types. Hence, you can use, among others, integers or symbols as type parameters.

The built-in `Array{T.N}` type is a good example of this usage. This type is parameterized by two parameters, one of which is a type and the other a value. The first parameter, `T`, is the type of the elements of the array. The second, `N`, is an integer specifying the number of dimensions of the array.

The addition of type parameters provides more information to the compiler about the composition of memory. For example, it allows the programmer to assert (or the compiler to infer) the types of elements stored within a container. This, as we'll discuss in the next section, allows the compiler to generate code in turn that is optimized to the types and storage in question.

Type inference

Types in Julia are optional and unobtrusive. The type system usually does not impede for the programmer. It is not necessary or recommended to annotate all variables with type information.

This is not to say that type information is redundant. Quite the opposite is true, in fact. A large part of Julia's speed comes from the ability of the compiler to compile and cache specialized versions of each function for all the possible types to which it can be applied. This means that most functions can be compiled down to their best possible optimized representations.

To achieve this balance, the runtime tries to figure out as much type information as it can through type inference. The algorithm is based on forward dataflow analysis. It should be noted that this is not an implementation of the famous Hindley-Milner algorithm using unification, which is used in the ML family of languages. In these languages, it is mandatory for the compiler to be able to determine the types of every value in the system. For Julia, however, the type inference can be performed on a best-effort basis, with any failure handled with a runtime fallback.

As a simple example of visible type inference, consider the following line of code that creates an array from a range of integers. This code does not have any type annotations. Yet the runtime is able to create an array with properly typed elements of Int64:

```
julia>[x for x=1:5]
5-element Array{Int64,1}:
 1
 2
 3
 4
 5
```

In this section, we provided a quick overview of some important type features in Julia. For more information, visit the online documentation at http://docs.julialang.org/en/release-0.4/manual/types/.

For the rest of this chapter, we will assume familiarity with these concepts and look at how this impacts the performance of Julia code

Type-stability

In order for the Julia compiler to compile a specialized version of functions for each different type of its argument, it needs to infer, as best as possible, the parameter and return types of all functions. Without this, Julia's speed would be hugely compromised. In order to do this effectively, the code must be written in a way that it is *type-stable*.

Definitions

Type-stability is the idea that the type of the return value of a function is dependent only on the types of its arguments and not the values. When this is true, the compiler can infer the return type of a function by knowing the types of its inputs. This ensures that type inference can continue across chains of function invocations without actually running the code, even though the language is fully dynamic.

As an example, let's look at the following code, which returns the input for positive numbers but 0 for negative numbers:

```
function trunc(x)
    if x < 0
        return 0
    else
        return x
    end
end
```

This code works for both integers and floating-point output, as follows:

```
julia> trunc(-1)
0


julia> trunc(-2.5)
0


julia> trunc(2.5)
2.5
```

However, you may notice an issue with calling this function with the float input. Take a look at the following:

```
julia> typeof(trunc(2.5))
Float64
```

```
julia> typeof(trunc(-2.5))
Int64
```

The return type of the `trunc` function, in this case, depends on the value of the input and not just its type. The type of the argument for both the preceding invocations is `Float64`. However, if the value of the input is less than zero, the type of the return is `Int64`. On the other hand, if the input is value is zero or greater, then the type of the output is `Float64`. This makes the function type-unstable.

Fixing type-instability

Now that we can recognize type-unstable code, the question arises: how can we fix code such as this? There are two obvious solutions. One would be to separate the write versions of the `trunc` function for different input types. So, we could have a version of `trunc` for integers and another for floating point. However, this would cause instances of repeated, copy-pasted code. Also, there would not be just two such instances; there would be copies for `Float32`, `Float64`, `Int32`, `Int64`, and so on. Further, we would have to write a new version of this function for all the new numeric types that are defined. It should be obvious that writing generic functions that operate on a wide variety of related types is really the best way to get concise and elegant Julia code.

The second obvious solution is to branch on the input type within the generic function. So, we could write code similar to this:

```
if typeof(x) == Float64
    return 0.0
elseif typeof(x) == Float32
    return Float32(0.0)
elseif typeof(x) == Int64
    return 0
......
end
```

I hope you can see that this can quickly get tedious. However, this type of code provides us with a hint to the correct solution. In Julia, whenever you find yourself explicitly checking the type of any variable, it is time to let dispatch do the job.

The Julia base library contains a `zero(x)` function that takes as its argument any numeric value and returns an appropriately typed zero value for this type. Using this function, we can write a generic `trunc` function that is type-stable yet works for any input type, as follows:

```
function trunc_fixed(x)
    if x < 0
```

```
            return zero(x)
        else
            return x
        end
    end
```

Output of the code:

```
julia> trunc_fixed(-2.4)
0.0

julia> trunc_fixed(-2)
0

julia> typeof(trunc_fixed(-2.4))
Float64

julia> typeof(trunc_fixed(-2))
Int64
```

In making the `trunc` function type-stable, we used a standard library function to move the type variable part of the code into another function. The principle applies when you do not have a base function to fall back upon. Isolate the part of your function that varies depending on the type of the input and allow Julia's dispatch to call the correct piece of code, depending on the type.

Performance pitfalls

We said that type-stability is very important for high-performance Julia code. The speed of Julia programs arises from its ability to compile and cache specialized code for each function argument type. When a function is type-unstable, the Julia compiler cannot compile a fast, specialized version of its caller. Let's take a look at this in action with the preceding code:

```
julia> @benchmark trunc(2.5)
================ Benchmark Results ========================
    Time per evaluation: 13.38 ns [13.04 ns, 13.73 ns]
Proportion of time in GC: 2.39% [1.76%, 3.01%]
        Memory allocated: 16.00 bytes
   Number of allocations: 1 allocations
       Number of samples: 13501
```

```
    Number of evaluations: 774542001
        R² of OLS model: 0.802
 Time spent benchmarking: 10.50 s



julia> @benchmark trunc_fixed(2.5)
================ Benchmark Results ========================
     Time per evaluation: 5.90 ns [5.86 ns, 5.94 ns]
 Proportion of time in GC: 0.00% [0.00%, 0.00%]
       Memory allocated: 0.00 bytes
   Number of allocations: 0 allocations
       Number of samples: 10601
    Number of evaluations: 48829501
        R² of OLS model: 0.985
 Time spent benchmarking: 0.51 s
```

Note that the type-stable version is twice as fast as the type-unstable version. Crucially, the type-stable version does not allocate any memory, while the type-unstable version does allocate quite a lot of memory. This combination of slow execution and large memory access is something that you will want to get rid of from your code at all times. Thankfully, it is not that hard to identify type-unstable tools. With the tools available within the language, you will be able to build up an intuition about this very quickly.

Identifying type-stability

In the preceding trunc function, the type instability was found by reading and understanding the code. In many cases where the code is longer or more complicated, it may not be easy or even possible to understand the type behavior of a function merely by inspection. It would be useful to have some tools at our disposal.

Fortunately, Julia provides the @code_warntype macro that enables us to view the types inferred by the compiler, thereby identifying any type instability in our code. The output of @code_warntype is the lowered, type-inferred AST structure. In other words, the compiler parses and processes the source code into a standardized form and then runs the type inference on the result to figure out the possible types of all the variables and function calls within the code.

Let's run this on our type-unstable method and take a look at what it says, as follows:

```
julia> @code_warntype trunc(2.5)
Variables:
  x::Float64
  ##fy#7786::Float64


Body:
  begin  # none, line 2:
      ##fy#7786 =
      (Base.box)(Float64,(Base.sitofp)(Float64,0))::Float64
      unless
(Base.box)(Base.Bool,(Base.or_int)((Base.lt_float)(x::Float64,##fy#77
86::Float64)::Bool,(Base.box)(Base.Bool,(Base.and_int)((Base.box)(Bas
e.Bool,(Base.and_int)((Base.eq_float)(x::Float64,##fy#7786::Float64):
:Bool,(Base.lt_float)(##fy#7786::Float64,9.223372036854776e18)::Bool)
::Any)::Bool,(Base.slt_int)((Base.box)(Int64,(Base.fptosi)(Int64,##fy
#7786::Float64))::Int64,0)::Bool)::Any)::Bool))::Bool goto 0 # none,
line 3:
      return 0
      goto 1
      0:  # none, line 5:
      return x::Float64
      1:
  end::UNION{FLOAT64,INT64}
```

While this output might look slightly scary at first, the relevant portions are easy to highlight. If you run this on Julia REPL, you will see that, in the last line of the output, "Union{Float64,Int64}", is highlighted in red (this is represented by capital letters in the preceding output). This line shows that the compiler inferred that the return type of this function, when passed Float64 as an argument, can either be Float64 or Int64. Therefore, this function is type-unstable, and this is made obvious by the red highlighting in REPL.

In general, the output from @code_warntype, as the name suggests, will warn us of any type inference problem in the code, highlighting it in red. These will usually be variables for which the compiler cannot infer any bound, those typed as ANY, or where there are multiple options for possible types denoted as Union. While there are some cases where these warnings might be false positives, they should always be investigated if they are unexpected.

If we run this macro on the `trunc_fixed` function, which we made type-stable, we will note that the compiler can infer `Float64` as the return type of the function. Upon running this in REPL, there is no red font in the output, giving us confidence that the function is type-stable. Take a look at the following:

```
julia> @code_warntype trunc_fixed(-2.4)
Variables:
  x::Float64
  ##fy#8904::Float64


Body:
  begin  # none, line 2:
      ##fy#8904 = (Base.box)(Float64,(Base.sitofp)
(Float64,0)::Any)::Float64

      unless

(Base.box)(Base.Bool,(Base.or_int)((Base.lt_float)(x::Float64,##fy#89
04::Float64)::Bool,(Base.box)(Base.Bool,(Base.and_int)((Base.box)(Bas
e.Bool,(Base.and_int)((Base.eq_float)(x::Float64,##fy#8904::Float64):
:Bool,(Base.lt_float)(##fy#8904::Float64,9.223372036854776e18)::Bool)
::Any)::Bool,(Base.slt_int)((Base.box)(Int64,(Base.fptosi)(Int64,##fy
#8904::Float64)::Any)::Int64,0)::Bool)::Any)::Bool)::Any)::Bool goto
0 # none, line 3:
      return (Base.box)(Float64,(Base.sitofp)(Float64,0)::Any)::Float64

      goto 1

      0:  # none, line 5:

      return x::Float64

      1:

  end::Float64
```

Further evidence of the benefits of type-stability can be observed by looking at the LLVM bitcode produced by the Julia compiler. This can be seen using the `@code_llvm` macro, which outputs the result of compiling Julia code into LLVM bitcode. While the details of the output are not relevant, it should be obvious that the type-stable function compiles a much smaller amount of code. It comprises fewer instructions and thus is significantly faster. Take a look at the following code:

```
julia> @code_llvm trunc(2.5)


define %jl_value_t* @julia_trunc_23088(double) {
top:
  %1 = fcmp uge double %0, 0.000000e+00
```

```
  br i1 %1, label %L, label %if


if:                                              ; preds = %top
  ret %jl_value_t* inttoptr (i64 4356202576 to %jl_value_t*)


L:                                               ; preds = %top
  %2 = call %jl_value_t* @jl_gc_alloc_1w()
  %3 = getelementptr inbounds %jl_value_t* %2, i64 -1, i32 0
  store %jl_value_t* inttoptr (i64 4357097552 to %jl_value_t*),
  %jl_value_t** %3, align 8
  %4 = bitcast %jl_value_t* %2 to double*
  store double %0, double* %4, align 16
  ret %jl_value_t* %2
}


julia> @code_llvm trunc_fixed(2.5)

define double @julia_trunc_fixed_23089(double) {
top:
  %1 = fcmp uge double %0, 0.000000e+00
  br i1 %1, label %L, label %if


if:                                              ; preds = %top
  ret double 0.000000e+00


L:                                               ; preds = %top
  ret double %0
}
```

If you are more comfortable with assembly instructions than with LLVM bitcode, the same inference can be gleaned from looking at the final assembly instructions that the Julia code compiles to. This can be output using the `@code_native` macro and is the final code that gets run on the computer's processor. This output is the result of the full gamut of compiler optimizations implemented by the Julia compiler as well as LLVM's JIT. Looking at the output for our usual functions, we can see once again that the type-stable function does significantly less work, as follows:

```
julia> @code_native trunc(2.5)
    .section    __TEXT,__text,regular,pure_instructions
Filename: none
Source line: 5
    pushq   %rbp
    movq    %rsp, %rbp
    subq    $16, %rsp
    vmovsd  %xmm0, -8(%rbp)
    vxorpd  %xmm1, %xmm1, %xmm1
    vucomisd    %xmm0, %xmm1
    ja    L67
Source line: 5
    movabsq   $jl_gc_alloc_1w, %rax
    callq   *%rax
    movabsq   $4357097552, %rcx        ## imm = 0x103B40850
    movq    %rcx, -8(%rax)
    vmovsd  -8(%rbp), %xmm0
    vmovsd  %xmm0, (%rax)
    jmpq    L77
L67:    movabsq   $4356202576, %rax   ## imm = 0x103A66050
Source line: 3
L77:    addq    $16, %rsp
    popq    %rbp
    ret


julia> @code_native trunc_fixed(2.5)
    .section    __TEXT,__text,regular,pure_instructions
Filename: none
Source line: 5
    pushq   %rbp
    movq    %rsp, %rbp
    vxorpd  %xmm1, %xmm1, %xmm1
    vucomisd    %xmm0, %xmm1
    jbe   L22
    vxorpd  %xmm0, %xmm0, %xmm0
Source line: 5
L22:    popq    %rbp
    ret
```

Loop variables

Another facet of type-stability that is important in Julia is that variables within a loop should not change their type from one iteration of the loop to another. Let's first look at a case where this is not true, as follows:

```
function sumsqrtn(n)
    r = 0
    for i = 1:n
        r = r + sqrt(i)
    end
    return r
end
```

In this function, the r variable starts out as Int64, when the loop is entered in the first iteration. However the sqrt function returns Float64, which when added to Int64, returns Float64. At this point, at Line 4 of the function, r becomes Float64. This violates the rule of not changing the type of a variable within a loop and makes this code type-unstable.

Inspecting the @code_warntype output for this function makes this obvious. Viewing this in REPL, we're faced with a swathe of red, which again is highlighted in capital letters here:

```
julia> @code_warntype sumsqrtn(5)
Variables:
  n::Int64
  r::ANY
  #s52::Int64
  i::Int64


Body:
  begin  # none, line 2:
      r = 0 # none, line 3:
      GenSym(0) = $(Expr(:new, UnitRange{Int64}, 1,
:(((top(getfield))(Base.Intrinsics,:select_value)::I)((Base.sle_int)(
1,n::Int64)::Bool,n::Int64,(Base.box)(Int64,(Base.sub_int)(1,1))::Int
64)::Int64)))
      #s52 = (top(getfield))(GenSym(0),:start)::Int64
      unless (Base.box)(Base.Bool,(Base.not_int)(#s52::Int64 ===
(Base.box)(Base.Int,(Base.add_int)((top(getfield))(GenSym(0),:stop)::
Int64,1))::Int64::Bool))::Bool goto 1
      2:
```

```
    GenSym(2) = #s52::Int64

    GenSym(3) =
(Base.box)(Base.Int,(Base.add_int)(#s52::Int64,1))::Int64

    i = GenSym(2)

    #s52 = GenSym(3) # none, line 4:

    r = r::Union{Float64,Int64} +
(Base.Math.box)(Base.Math.Float64,(Base.Math.sqrt_llvm)((Base.box)(Fl
oat64,(Base.sitofp)(Float64,i::Int64))::Float64))::Float64::Float64

    3:

    unless
(Base.box)(Base.Bool,(Base.not_int)((Base.box)(Base.Bool,(Base.not_in
t)(#s52::Int64 ===
(Base.box)(Base.Int,(Base.add_int)((top(getfield))(GenSym(0),:stop)::
Int64,1))::Int64::Bool))::Bool))::Bool goto 2

    1:

    0:  # none, line 6:

    return r::UNION{FLOAT64,INT64}
end::UNION{FLOAT64,INT64}
```

This output shows that the compiler cannot infer a tight bound for the value of r (it is typed as ANY), and the function itself can return either Float64 or Int64 (for example, it is typed as Union{Float64,Int64})

Fixing the instability is easy in this case. We just need to initialize the r variable to be the Float64 value as we know that that is the type it will eventually take. Take a look at the following function now:

```
function sumsqrtn_fixed(n)
    r = 0.0
    for i = 1:n
        r = r + sqrt(i)
    end
    return r
end
```

The @code_warntype output for this function is now clean, as follows:

```
julia> @code_warntype sumsqrtn_fixed(5)
Variables:
  n::Int64
  r::Float64
  #s52::Int64
```

```
    i::Int64


Body:
  begin  # none, line 2:
      r = 0.0 # none, line 3:
      GenSym(0) = $(Expr(:new, UnitRange{Int64}, 1,
:(((top(getfield))(Base.Intrinsics,:select_value)::I)((Base.sle_int)(
1,n::Int64)::Bool,n::Int64,(Base.box)(Int64,(Base.sub_int)(1,1))::Int
64)::Int64)))
      #s52 = (top(getfield))(GenSym(0),:start)::Int64
      unless (Base.box)(Base.Bool,(Base.not_int)(#s52::Int64 ===
(Base.box)(Base.Int,(Base.add_int)((top(getfield))(GenSym(0),:stop)::
Int64,1))::Int64::Bool))::Bool goto 1
      2:
      GenSym(2) = #s52::Int64
      GenSym(3) =
(Base.box)(Base.Int,(Base.add_int)(#s52::Int64,1))::Int64
      i = GenSym(2)
      #s52 = GenSym(3) # none, line 4:
      r =
(Base.box)(Base.Float64,(Base.add_float)(r::Float64,(Base.Math.box)(B
ase.Math.Float64,(Base.Math.sqrt_llvm)((Base.box)(Float64,(Base.sitof
p)(Float64,i::Int64))::Float64))::Float64))::Float64
      3:
      unless
(Base.box)(Base.Bool,(Base.not_int)((Base.box)(Base.Bool,(Base.not_in
t)(#s52::Int64 ===
(Base.box)(Base.Int,(Base.add_int)((top(getfield))(GenSym(0),:stop)::
Int64,1))::Int64::Bool))::Bool))::Bool goto 2
      1:
      0:  # none, line 6:
      return r::Float64
  end::Float64
```

To show why all of this is important, let's time both of these functions, as follows:

```
julia> @benchmark sumsqrtn(1000_000)
================ Benchmark Results =========================
    Time per evaluation: 36.26 ms [34.02 ms, 38.49 ms]
Proportion of time in GC: 18.81% [15.57%, 22.05%]
        Memory allocated: 30.52 mb
```

```
    Number of allocations: 2000000 allocations
       Number of samples: 100
   Number of evaluations: 100
Time spent benchmarking: 3.80 s


julia> @benchmark sumsqrtn_fixed(1000_000)
================ Benchmark Results ========================
        Time per evaluation: 9.52 ms [9.05 ms, 9.99 ms]
Proportion of time in GC: 0.00% [0.00%, 0.00%]
       Memory allocated: 0.00 bytes
   Number of allocations: 0 allocations
       Number of samples: 100
   Number of evaluations: 100
Time spent benchmarking: 0.98 s
```

Here, we can see that the type-stable version is four times as fast. More importantly, the type-unstable version of the function allocates a large amount of memory, which is unnecessary. Using type-unstable code, therefore, is extremely prejudicial to high-performance code.

Kernel methods

Type inference in Julia primarily works by inspecting the types of function parameters and identifying the type of the return value. This suggests that some type instability issues may be mitigated by breaking up a function into smaller functions. This can provide additional hints to the compiler, making more accurate type inferencing possible.

For an example of this, consider a contrived function that takes as input the "Int64" or "Float64" string and returns an array of 10 elements, the types of which correspond to the type name passed as the input argument. Functions such as this may arise when creating arrays based on user input or by reading a file in which the type of the output is determined at runtime. Take a look at the following:

```
function string_zeros(s::AbstractString)
    x = Array(s=="Int64"?Int64:Float64, 1_000_000)
    for i in 1:length(x)
        x[i] = 0
    end
    return x
end
```

We will benchmark this code to find an average execution time of over 38 milliseconds per function call with a large memory allocation, as shown by the following code:

```
julia> @benchmark string_zeros("Int64")
================ Benchmark Results ========================
     Time per evaluation: 38.05 ms [36.80 ms, 39.30 ms]
Proportion of time in GC: 6.45% [6.07%, 6.83%]
       Memory allocated: 22.88 mb
   Number of allocations: 999492 allocations
       Number of samples: 100
   Number of evaluations: 100
Time spent benchmarking: 4.19 s
```

This seems to be unnecessarily high. The loop in the function is the obvious place where most of the time is spent within this function. We note that, in this loop, the type of the variable being accessed (x) cannot be known before the function is called, even when the type of the function arguments is known. This prevents the compiler from generating an optimized loop operating on one specific type.

What we need to do is ensure that the loop operates in such a way that the type of the x variable is known to the compiler. As we said earlier, type inference operates on function boundaries, which suggests a solution to our conundrum. We can split out the loop into its own function, separating the determination of the type of x and the operations on x across a function call, as follows:

```
function string_zeros_stable(s::AbstractString)
  x = Array(s=="Int64"?Int64:Float64, 1_000_000)
  return fill_zeros(x)
end

function fill_zeros(x)
  for i in 1:length(x)
    x[i] = 0
  end
  return x
end
```

Now, by benchmarking this solution, we will find that the execution time of our function reduces by a factor of 10, with a corresponding fall in the allocated memory. Therefore, in situations where the types of variables are uncertain, we need to be careful in ensuring that the compiler can be provided with as much information as necessary.

Types in storage locations

We discussed in the earlier sections that, when writing idiomatic Julia code, we should try and write functions with the minimum amount of type constraints possible in order to write generic code. We do not need to specify the types of function arguments or local variables for performance reasons. The compiler will be able to infer the required types. Thus, while the types are important, they are usually optional when writing Julia code. In general, bindings do not need to be typed; they are inferred.

However, when defining storage locations for data, it is important to specify a concrete type. So, for things that hold data, such as arrays, dictionaries, or fields in composite types, it is best to explicitly define the type that it will hold.

Arrays

As an example, let's create two arrays containing the same data — the numbers one to ten, which are of the Int64 type. The first array we will create is defined to hold values of the Int64 type. The second is defined to hold values of the abstract Number type, which is a supertype of Int64. Take a look at the following code:

```
julia> a = Int64[1, 2, 3, 4, 5, 6, 7, 8, 9, 10]
10-element Array{Int64,1}:
   1
   2
   3
   4
   5
   6
   7
   8
   9
  10

julia> b = Number[1,2,3,4,5,6,7,8,9,10]
10-element Array{Number,1}:
   1
   2
   3
   4
```

```
 5
 6
 7
 8
 9
10
```

We will then pass these arrays into the following function that calculates the sum of squares of the elements of these arrays, as follows:

```
function arr_sumsqr{T <: Number}(x::Array{T})
    r = zero(T)
    for i = 1:length(x)
        r = r + x[i] ^ 2
    end
    return r
end
```

By timing the invocations, we will see that, when using the Int64 array, this computation is over ten times faster than when using the Number array, even when the data within the arrays is identical, as follows:

```
julia> @benchmark arr_sumsqr(a)
================= Benchmark Results =======================
     Time per evaluation: 34.52 ns [34.06 ns, 34.99 ns]
Proportion of time in GC: 0.00% [0.00%, 0.00%]
       Memory allocated: 0.00 bytes
   Number of allocations: 0 allocations
       Number of samples: 9301
   Number of evaluations: 14145701
        R² of OLS model: 0.955
 Time spent benchmarking: 0.54 s


julia> @benchmark arr_sumsqr(b)
================= Benchmark Results =======================
     Time per evaluation: 463.24 ns [455.46 ns, 471.02 ns]
Proportion of time in GC: 0.00% [0.00%, 0.00%]
       Memory allocated: 0.00 bytes
   Number of allocations: 0 allocations
       Number of samples: 6601
```

```
Number of evaluations: 1080001
       R² of OLS model: 0.951
Time spent benchmarking: 0.57 s
```

The reason for this massive difference lies in how the values are stored within the array. When the array is defined to contain a specific concrete type, the Julia runtime can store the values inline within the allocation of the array since it knows the exact size of each element. When the array can contain an abstract type, the actual value can be of any size. Thus, when the Julia runtime creates the array, it only stores the pointers to the actual values within the array. The values are stored elsewhere on the heap. This not only causes an extra memory load when reading the values, the indirection can mess up pipelining and cache affinity when executing this code on the CPU.

Composite types

There is another situation where concrete types must be specified for good performance: in the fields of composite types.

As an example, consider a composite type holding the location of a point in 2D space. In this scenario, we could define the object as follows:

```
immutable Point
    x
    y
end
```

However, this definition would perform quite badly. The primary issue is that the x and y fields in this type can be used to store values of any type. In particular, they could be other complex types that are accessed as pointers. In this case, the compiler will not know whether access to the fields of the Point type requires a pointer indirection, and thus it cannot optimize the reading of these values.

It will be much better to define this type with the field values constrained to concrete types. This will have two benefits. Firstly, the field values will be stored inline when the object is allocated rather than being not directed via pointer. Secondly, all code that uses fields of this type will be able to be type-inferred correctly, as follows:

```
immutable ConcretePoint
    x::Float64
    y::Float64
end
```

Parametric composite types

While the preceding definition of ConcretePoint performs well, it loses some significant flexibility. If we wanted to store the field values as Float32 or Float16, we would be unable to use the same type. To lose so much flexibility for performance seems very unfortunate.

It would be tempting to fix this using an abstract type as the fields. In this case, all the concrete floating point numbers are subtypes of the AbstractFloat type. Here, we could then define a PointsWithAbstract type that contains fields annotated as AbstractFloat, as follows:

```
immutable PointWithAbstract
    x::AbstractFloat
    y::AbstractFloat
end
```

However, this code has the same drawbacks as the original Point type mentioned earlier. It will be slow, and the compiler will be unable to optimize access to the type. The solution is to use a parametric type, as follows:

```
function ParametricPoint{T <: AbstractFloat}
    x::T
    y::T
end
```

When we write the type in this manner, our code remains generic. We can write our methods with the confidence that the ParametricPoint type can hold values for any type of a floating point number. Yet, at runtime, when an instance of this type is created, it is instantiated with a particular type of float. In other words, once an instance is created, T becomes known. At this point, all the benefits of specifying the concrete type discussed before are applicable. Both storage and type inferences are efficient now.

Summary

In this chapter, we discussed how types play a crucial role in writing idiomatic and performant code in Julia. Much of what we discussed here is exactly what makes Julia unique—a dynamic language where types, dispatch, and inference play a fundamental role.

We discussed how to write type-stable code and when and how to define type annotations for performance. In the next chapter, we will discuss the performance characteristics of another important part of the language: functions.

4
Functions and Macros – Structuring Julia Code for High Performance

In Julia, the function is the primary unit of a code structure. Idiomatic Julia code consists of many small functions that are defined with different types of arguments. In general, the overhead of a function call in Julia is very small, and, with type specialization, the compiled version of the function is very efficient. In this chapter, we will look at some of the techniques that Julia uses to make function calls very fast. We will also look at some limitations that are worth keeping in mind for the fastest code. Finally, we will look at some situations where moving code out of functions and into other structures, such as macros and staged functions, allows code to be faster and more efficient:

- Using globals
- Inlining
- Closures and anonymous functions
- Using macros for performance
- Using generated functions
- Using named parameters

Using globals

One of the first performance tips that you come across when learning Julia is the advice not to use global variables. This is usually not a very onerous requirement, as global state is often considered bad programming practice. Further, this limitation is most likely going to be removed in future versions of Julia. However, given how easy it is to fall into this trap and the large amount of performance degradation that can occur, it is important to keep this in mind when writing Julia code.

The trouble with globals

In the previous chapter, we saw how Julia achieves its high performance runtime by compiling specialized versions of functions for particular types of arguments—a process that relies on type inference using data flow techniques. However, global variables can be written to at any time, and by any code. The compiler cannot keep track of all writes to global variables; this would be akin to solving the halting problem. Therefore, the data-flow technique fails to perform any inference for these types of global variables. As a result, the compiler cannot create specialized functions when using these variables.

To understand the performance hit of using global variables, let's use a simple function that calculates the sum of the integer powers of a set of floating point values. We use a global variable to store the integer power:

```
p = 2

function pow_array(x::Vector{Float64})
    s = 0.0
    for y in x
        s = s + y^p
    end
    return s
end
```

Benchmarking this function, we see that it takes approximately 10 milliseconds for each evaluation of this function for an input array of length `100000`. This is way too high for something that should only take a few machine instructions to execute:

```
julia> t=rand(100000);

julia> @benchmark pow_array(t)
================ Benchmark Results ========================
       Time per evaluation: 9.39 ms [8.48 ms, 10.30 ms]
 Proportion of time in GC: 4.58% [0.00%, 10.14%]
         Memory allocated: 4.58 mb
     Number of allocations: 300000 allocations
         Number of samples: 100
     Number of evaluations: 100
  Time spent benchmarking: 0.97 s
```

A look at the `@code_warntype` output for this function shows us that the compiler has been unable to infer the type of the result when calculating with the global variable, marking it as ANY. This then flows through the entire function, right up to the return value (as usual, any untyped variables, displayed in red in the REPL, are shown in capital letters, as follows):

```
julia> @code_warntype pow_array(t)

Variables:
  x::Array{Float64,1}
  s::ANY
  #s641::Int64
  y::Float64

Body:
  begin  # none, line 2:
      s = 0.0 # none, line 3:
      #s641 = 1
      GenSym(2) = (Base.arraylen)(x::Array{Float64,1})::Int64
      unless
(Base.box)(Base.Bool,(Base.not_int)((Base.slt_int)(GenSym(2),#s641
::Int64)::Bool))::Bool goto 1
      2:
      GenSym(4) = (Base.arrayref)(x::Array{Float64,1},#s641::Int64)::Flo
at64
      GenSym(5) = (Base.box)(Base.Int,(Base.add_int)
(#s641::Int64,1)::Any)::Int64
      y = GenSym(4)
      #s641 = GenSym(5) # none, line 4:
      s = s + y::Float64 ^ Main.p::ANY::ANY
      3:
```

```
    GenSym(3) = (Base.arraylen)(x::Array{Float64,1})::Int64

    unless
(Base.box)(Base.Bool,(Base.not_int)((Base.box)(Base.Bool,(Base.not
_int)((Base.slt_int)(GenSym(3),#s641::Int64)::Bool))::Bool))::Bool
goto 2

    1:

    0:  # none, line 6:

    return s
  end:: ANY
```

Fixing performance issues with globals

A simple way to get back performance is to declare the global variable a `const`:

```
const p2 = 2
function pow_array2(x::Vector{Float64})
  s = 0.0
    for y in x
        s = s + y^p2
    end
    return s
end
```

Just this change will get us a little under two orders of magnitude performance gain on the following function:

```
julia> @benchmark pow_array2(t)
================ Benchmark Results ========================
    Time per evaluation: 123.90 µs [120.54 µs, 127.27 µs]
Proportion of time in GC: 0.00% [0.00%, 0.00%]
        Memory allocated: 0.00 bytes
    Number of allocations: 0 allocations
        Number of samples: 3901
    Number of evaluations: 82201
          R² of OLS model: 0.926
 Time spent benchmarking: 10.44 s
```

Global const

The const declaration in Julia means something different from the similar keyword in C. In Julia, a global variable declared as const can change its value (a warning is printed). However, what it cannot do is change its type. Also, note that you cannot explicitly declare the type of a global variable. That is, an incantation, such as x::Int64 = 2, will raise an error when made in the global scope.

Once again, @code_warntype will show us that this function is now correctly type inferred all the way through. Compare this output against the one from the previous function in the preceding section. You will notice that the return value of this function is being inferred as Float64:

```
julia> @code_warntype pow_array2(t)
Variables:
  x::Array{Float64,1}
  s::Float64
  #s614::Int64
  y::Float64


Body:
  begin  # none, line 2:
      s = 0.0 # none, line 3:
      #s614 = 1
      GenSym(2) = (Base.arraylen)(x::Array{Float64,1})::Int64
      unless (Base.box)(Base.Bool,(Base.not_int)((Base.slt_int)(GenSym(2)
,#s614::Int64)::Bool))::Bool goto 1
      2:
      GenSym(4) = (Base.arrayref)(x::Array{Float64,1},#s614::Int64)::Flo
at64
      GenSym(5) = (Base.box)(Base.Int,(Base.add_int)
(#s614::Int64,1))::Int64
      y = GenSym(4)
      #s614 = GenSym(5) # none, line 4:
      s = (Base.box)(Base.Float64,(Base.add_float)(s::Float64,(Base.
Math.box)(Base.Math.Float64,(Base.Math.powi_llvm)(y::Float64,(Base.box)
(Int32,(Base.checked_trunc_sint)(Int32,Main.p2))::Int32))::Float64))::Flo
at64
```

```
    3:
    GenSym(3) = (Base.arraylen)(x::Array{Float64,1})::Int64
    unless (Base.box)(Base.Bool,(Base.not_int)((Base.box)(Base.
Bool,(Base.not_int)((Base.slt_int)(GenSym(3),#s614::Int64)::Bool))::Bool)
)::Bool goto 2
    1:
    0:  # none, line 6:
    return s::Float64
  end::Float64
```

Another way to solve the issue of the global variable is to pass the global as a function argument. A function argument can be type inferred; hence, the function specialization will be effected in this case.

Inlining

As we've mentioned before, Julia code consists of many small functions. Unlike most other language implementations, some of the core primitives in the base library are also implemented in Julia. This means that the function call overhead has the potential to be a bottleneck in a Julia program. This is mitigated using some aggressive inlining performed by the Julia compiler.

Inlining is an optimization performed by a compiler, where the contents of a function or method is inserted directly into the body of the caller of that function. Thus, instead of making a function call, execution continues directly by executing the operations of the callee within the caller's body.

In addition, many compiler optimization techniques work within the body of a single function. Inlining, therefore, allows many more optimizations to be effective within the program.

Compiler optimizations

Julia uses the LLVM compiler to generate machine code, which is finally run on the CPU. Most of the usual compiler optimization techniques that run on Julia code are performed by LLVM. The one major exception is inlining, which is performed by the Julia compiler itself before LLVM is invoked.

Default inlining

The Julia compiler automatically inlines functions that it considers inline-worthy. The compiler implements a set of heuristics to determine what to inline. Essentially, this boils down to small functions with deterministic types.

 While inlining usually results in an increase in code speed, it also simultaneously increases the size of the code. Hence, a balance needs to be maintained. The heuristics are, therefore, tuned to maximize the performance of typical Julia code without causing excessive bloating of the compiled code.

As an example, let's take a look at a simple set of functions, some of which we've seen in previous chapters:

```
trunc(x) = x < 0 ? zero(x) : x

function sqrt_sin(x)
    y = trunc(x)
    return sin(sqrt(y)+1)
end
```

We can then look at the processed AST after the compiler has run its type inference and inlining passes. Note how in the following output, the code for the `trunc` function has been inserted into the `sqrt_sin` function as the first few lines:

```
julia> @code_typed sqrt_sin(1)
1-element Array{Any,1}:
 :($(Expr(:lambda, Any[:x],
Any[Any[Any[:x,Int64,0],Any[:y,Int64,18],Any[:_var0,Int64,2]],Any[
],Any[Float64,Float64,Float64],Any[]], :(begin  # none, line 2:
        unless (Base.slt_int)(x::Int64,0)::Bool goto 1
        _var0 = 0
        goto 2
        1:
        _var0 = x::Int64
        2:
        y = _var0::Int64 # none, line 3:
        GenSym(0) = (Base.box)(Base.Float64,(Base.add_float)((Base.Math.
box)(Base.Math
.Float64,(Base.Math.sqrt_llvm)((Base.box)(Float64,(Base.sitofp)(Float64,y
::Int64))::Float64))::Float64,(Base.box)(Float64,(Base.sito
fp)(Float64,1))::Float64))::Float64
```

```
     GenSym(2) =
(top(ccall))((top(tuple))("sin",Base.Math.libm)::Tuple{ASCIIString
,ASCIIString},Base.Math.Float64,(top(svec))(Base.Math.Float64)::Si
mpleVector,GenSym(0),0)::Float64

     return
 (Base.Math.nan_dom_err)(GenSym(2),GenSym(0))::Float64
   end::Float64))))
```

Controlling inlining

Sometimes, the heuristics to inline that are built into the Julia compiler will fail to inline functions that we want inlined. These would typically be performance-sensitive functions that are called many times in inner loops, for example, array indexers. For this purpose, Julia provides the `@inline` macro. This macro needs to be placed in front of a function definition. When that function is called, its body will be placed inline at the location where it is called.

 There is no call-site annotation to force inlining. We cannot inline a particular invocation of an, otherwise, normal function. The function itself should be marked with `@inline`, and then every invocation of that function will be inlined.

Let's demonstrate this with an example. In the following code, we define an `f(x)` function that performs some numerical operations on its arguments, as well as a `g(x)` function that calls `f` after transforming its argument:

```
function f(x)
    a=x*5
    b=a+3
    c=a-4
    d=b/c
end
```

This function `f` is too long to be inlined by default, which we verify by inspecting the `@code_typed` output of its `g` calling function. Note that the function definition of `g` continues to contain a call to the `f` function:

```
julia> @code_typed g(3)
1-element Array{Any,1}:
 :($(Expr(:lambda, Any[:x],
Any[Any[Any[:x,Int64,0]],Any[],Any[],Any[]], :(begin  # none, line 1:
```

```
    return
(Main.f)((Base.box)(Int64,(Base.mul_int)(2,x::Int64))::Int64)::Fl
oat64
    end::Float64))))
```

We then define the same computation in a function that we declare with the `@inline` macro:

```
@inline function f_inline(x)
    a=x*5
    b=a+3
    c=a-4
    d=b/c
end


g_inline(x) = f_inline(2*x)
```

When we inspect the compiled AST for this function, it is apparent that the called function has been inlined into the caller:

```
julia> @code_typed g_inline(3)
1-element Array{Any,1}:
 :($(Expr(:lambda, Any[:x], Any[Any[Any[:x,Int64,0],Any[symbol("##a#6865"
),Int64,18],Any[symbol("
##b#6866"),Int64,18],Any[symbol("##c#6867"),Int64,18],Any[symbol("##d
#6868"),Float64,18]],Any[],Any[Float64],Any[]], :(begin  # none, line
1:
        ##a#6865 =
(Base.box)(Int64,(Base.mul_int)((Base.box)(Int64,(Base.mul_int)(2,x::
Int64))::Int64,5))::Int64
        ##b#6866 =
(Base.box)(Base.Int,(Base.add_int)(##a#6865::Int64,3))::Int64
        ##c#6867 =
(Base.box)(Int64,(Base.sub_int)(##a#6865::Int64,4))::Int64
        GenSym(0) =
(Base.box)(Base.Float64,(Base.div_float)((Base.box)(Float64,(Base.sit
ofp)(Float64,##b#6866::Int64))::Float64,(Base.box)(Float64,(Base.sito
fp)(Float64,##c#6867::Int64))::Float64))::Float64
        ##d#6868 = GenSym(0)
        return GenSym(0)
    end::Float64))))
```

It is even more instructive to see the LLVM bitcode that is generated from this function. We can see this using the `@code_llvm` macro. Note that the first line of the function is now `%1 = mul i64 %0, 10`. This shows the argument of the function being multiplied by 10. Look back at the source of the function — the argument is multiplied by `2` in the `g` function and, subsequently, by `5` in the `f` function. The LLVM optimizer has recognized this and consolidated these two operations into a single multiplication. This optimization has occurred by merging code across two different functions and, thus, couldn't have happened without inlining:

```
julia> @code_llvm g_inline(3)

define double @julia_g_inline_21456(i64) {
top:
  %1 = mul i64 %0, 10
  %2 = add i64 %1, 3
  %3 = add i64 %1, -4
  %4 = sitofp i64 %2 to double
  %5 = sitofp i64 %3 to double
  %6 = fdiv double %4, %5
  ret double %6
}
```

Disabling inlining

We've seen how useful inlining can be for the performance of our programs. However, in some situations, it may be useful to turn off all inlining. These can be during complex debugging sessions or while running code coverage analysis. For example, in any situation where one needs to maintain direct correspondence between source lines of code and executing machine code, inlining can be problematic.

Therefore, Julia provides a `-inline=no` command line option to be used in these circumstances. Using this option will disable all inlining, including the ones marked with `@inline`. We warned you that using this option makes all Julia code significantly slower. However, in rare situations this is exactly what is needed.

Closures and anonymous functions

We saw how important functions are in idiomatic Julia code. While not a pure functional language, Julia shares many features with such languages. In particular, functions in Julia are first class entities, and they can passed around to other functions to create higher-order functions. A canonical example of such a higher-order function is the map function, which evaluates the given function over each element of the provided collection.

As you would expect from a language with these functional features, it is also possible to create closures and anonymous functions in Julia. Anonymous functions, as the name suggests, are functions without a name, and they are usually created at the point where they are passed in to another function as an argument. In Julia, they are created with the -> operator separating the arguments from the function body. These, and named functions created within the scope of another function, and referring to variables from this outer scope, are called closures. This name arises from the idea of these functions "closing over" the outer scope.

Anonymous functions and closures are much slower than named functions in versions of Julia prior to *0.5*. This is due to the fact that the Julia compiler currently cannot type infer the result of anonymous functions. It should be obvious that the lack of type inference will significantly slow these functions down. As always, it is instructive to look at an example and measure its performance. First, we define a sqr function, which returns the square of its input argument:

```
sqr(x) = x ^ 2
```

We then measure the performance of map, evaluating this function over a random array of 100,000 Float64 elements. We also measure the performance of map when it is passed the same computation as an anonymous function, rather than the named sqr function:

```
julia> @benchmark map(sqr, rand(100_000))
================ Benchmark Results ========================
       Time per evaluation: 3.81 ms [2.98 ms, 4.64 ms]
Proportion of time in GC: 8.88% [0.00%, 20.33%]
        Memory allocated: 3.81 mb
    Number of allocations: 200003 allocations
        Number of samples: 100
    Number of evaluations: 100
 Time spent benchmarking: 0.41 s
```

```
julia> @benchmark map(x->x^2, rand(100_000))
================ Benchmark Results ========================
        Time per evaluation: 7.97 ms [6.97 ms, 8.96 ms]
Proportion of time in GC: 5.38% [0.00%, 12.70%]
        Memory allocated: 3.81 mb
    Number of allocations: 200003 allocations
        Number of samples: 100
    Number of evaluations: 100
 Time spent benchmarking: 0.83 s
```

It is apparent that using a named function is about twice as fast as using an anonymous function. It should be noted that while this is true of the current version of Julia at the time of writing (0.4,) this limitation will be removed in future versions of Julia. If you are using Julia v0.5 or later, then you do not need to consider any of the content in this section or the next section. In these versions, anonymous functions are as fast as named functions. However, for the moment, it is advisable to limit uses of closures and anonymous functions as much as possible in performance-sensitive code.

FastAnonymous

However, in many situations, it is necessary or even convenient to use anonymous functions. We have a language with many functional features, and it would be a shame to forgo closures. So, if the slow performance of these constructs are a bottleneck in your code, the innovative Julia community has a workaround in the form of the FastAnonymous package.

Using this package is easy and causes very low programmer overhead. After installing and importing, writing an @anon macro before an anonymous function declaration will transform it into a form that can be type inferred, and this is, thus, much faster. Running the example from the previous section with this approach yields a significantly faster runtime:

```
julia> using FastAnonymous
```

```
julia> @benchmark map(@anon(x->x^2), rand(100_000))
```

```
================ Benchmark Results ========================
    Time per evaluation: 488.63 µs [298.53 µs, 678.73 µs]
Proportion of time in GC: 0.00% [0.00%, 0.00%]
      Memory allocated: 781.31 kb
  Number of allocations: 2 allocations
      Number of samples: 100
  Number of evaluations: 100
 Time spent benchmarking: 0.29 s
```

Once again, we should note that use of this package will become unnecessary in version 0.5 and further versions of Julia when the performance difference between anonymous and named functions are removed.

Using macros for performance

So far in this chapter, we have focused on making our functions run faster. However, as fast we make them, all the computation occurs when a function is called. The best way to make any code faster is, however, to do less work. So, a strategy is to move any possible work to compile time, which leaves less work to do at runtime.

The Julia compilation process

However, for a dynamic language such as Julia, the terms compile time and runtime are not always clearly defined. In some sense, everything happens at runtime because our code is not compiled to a binary ahead of time. However, there are clearly divided processes that occur from when the code is read from disk to when it is finally executed on the CPU.

As the compiler goes through each stage, it can write code to execute at various points along this pipeline rather than everything waiting until the end—the runtime. While we might loosely use the terminology of compile time for some of our metaprogramming techniques, having the ability to run code at multiple stages along this pipeline provides some powerful capabilities:

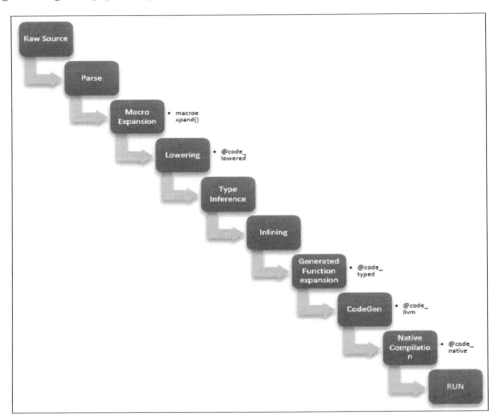

Using macros

Julia macros are code that can be used to write Julia code. A macro is executed very early in the compiler process, as soon as the code is loaded and parsed.

Macros are usually used as a means to reduce repetitive code, whereby large volumes of code with a common pattern can be generated from a smaller set of primitives. However, they can also be used to improve performance in some situations. This usually involves moving common or constant computation to the compile time wherever possible. To see how this can work, let's look at the problem of evaluating a polynomial.

Evaluating a polynomial

Consider the following polynomial expression:

$$p(x) = \sum_{i=0}^{n} a_i x^i = a_0 + a_1 x + a_2 x^2 + a_3 x^3 + \cdots + a_n x^n$$

Given a set of coefficients $[a_0, a_1, a_2, \ldots, a_n]$, we need to find the value of the $p(x)$ function for a particular value of x.

A simple and naive but general implementation to evaluate any polynomial may be, as follows:

```
function poly_naive(x, a...)
  p=zero(x)
  for i = 1:length(a)
    p = p + a[i]  *  x^(i-1)
  end
  return p
end
```

Type Stability, once again

You will recognize this from the discussions in the previous chapter that the initialization of p=zero(x) rather than p=0 ensures the type stability of this code.

Using this function, let's imagine that we need to compute a particular polynomial:

$$f(x) = 1 + 2x + 3x^2 + 4x^3 + 5x^4$$

```
julia> f_naive(x) = poly_naive(x, 1,2,3,4,5)
```

```
julia> f_naive(3.5)
966.5625
```

Let's verify the calculation by hand to test its accuracy and then benchmark the computation to see how fast it can run:

```
julia>  1 + 2*3.5 + 3*3.5^2 + 4*3.5^3 + 5*3.5^4
966.5625
```

```
julia> @benchmark f_naive(3.5)
================ Benchmark Results ========================
    Time per evaluation: 162.51 ns [160.31 ns, 164.71 ns]
Proportion of time in GC: 0.18% [0.00%, 0.39%]
        Memory allocated: 32.00 bytes
   Number of allocations: 2 allocations
       Number of samples: 9701
   Number of evaluations: 20709801
         R² of OLS model: 0.953
 Time spent benchmarking: 3.39 s
```

This computation takes a little over 160 nanoseconds. While this is not a particularly long interval, it is quite long for modern CPUs. A 2.4 GHz processor should be able to perform around 10,000 floating point operations in that time, which seems like a lot of work to compute a polynomial with five terms. The primary reason why this is slower than we would expect is that floating-point exponentiation is a particularly expensive operation.

> **Peak Flops**
>
> The peakflops() Julia function will return the maximum number of **floating point operations per second (flops)** possible on the current processor.

Horner's method

So, the first thing to do is to find a better algorithm, one which can replace the exponentiation into multiplications. This can be done by the Horner method, which is named after the nineteenth century British mathematician, William George Horner. This is accomplished by defining a sequence, as follows:

$$b_n = a_n$$
$$b_{n-1} = a_{n-1} + b_n x$$
$$b_{n-2} = a_{n-2} + b_{n-1} x$$
$$\vdots$$
$$b_0 = a_0 + b_a x$$

Then, b_0 is the value of the $p(x)$ polynomial.

This algorithm can be implemented in Julia, as follows:

```
function poly_horner(x, a...)
  b=zero(x)
    for i = length(a):-1:1
      b = a[i] + b * x
    end
    return b
end
```

We can then test and benchmark this for the same polynomial:

```
f_horner(x) = poly_horner(x, 1,2,3,4,5)


julia> @benchmark f_horner(3.5)
================ Benchmark Results ========================
    Time per evaluation: 41.51 ns [40.96 ns, 42.06 ns]
Proportion of time in GC: 1.16% [0.75%, 1.57%]
        Memory allocated: 32.00 bytes
   Number of allocations: 2 allocations
        Number of samples: 12301
   Number of evaluations: 246795401
          R² of OLS model: 0.943
 Time spent benchmarking: 10.36 s
```

We see that using a better algorithm gets us a *4x* improvement in the evaluation speed of this polynomial. Can we do better?

The Horner macro

Improving the speed of this computation starts with realizing that the coefficients of the polynomial are constants. They do not change and are known when writing the program. In other words, they are known at compile time. So, maybe we can expand and write out the expression for the Horner's rule for our polynomial. This will take the following form, for the polynomial that we used previously:

```
muladd(x,muladd(x,muladd(x,muladd(x,5,4),3),2),1)
```

This is likely to be the fastest way to compute our polynomial. However, writing this out for every polynomial that we might want to use will be extremely annoying. We loose the benefit of having a general library function that can compute any polynomial.

This is exactly the kind of situation where macros can help. We can write a macro that will produce the previous expression when given a set of polynomial coefficients. This can be done when the compiler loads the code. At runtime, when this function is called, it will execute this optimized expression. Julia's base library contains this macro, which we can see repeated, as follows:

```
macro horner(x, p...)
    ex = esc(p[end])
    for i = length(p)-1:-1:1
        ex = :(muladd(t, $ex, $(esc(p[i]))))
    end
    Expr(:block, :(t = $(esc(x))), ex)
end


f_horner_macro(x) = @horner(x, 1,2,3,4,5)


julia> @benchmark f_horner_macro(3.5)
================ Benchmark Results ========================
    Time per evaluation: 3.66 ns [3.62 ns, 3.69 ns]
Proportion of time in GC: 0.00% [0.00%, 0.00%]
      Memory allocated: 0.00 bytes
  Number of allocations: 0 allocations
      Number of samples: 11601
  Number of evaluations: 126646601
        R² of OLS model: 0.970
 Time spent benchmarking: 0.53 s
```

So, this method using a macro gives us an amazing *10x* improvement over calling the Horner's method as a function. Also, this function does not allocate any memory at runtime.

We've seen how this strategy of generating customized code for particular problems using a macro can sometimes lead to massive performance increases. While the @ horner macro is a simple and canonical example of this strategy, it can be used to great effect in our own code.

Generated functions

Macros run very early in the compilers process when there is no information about how the program might execute. The inputs to a macro are, therefore, simply symbols and expressions—the textual tokens that make up a program. Given that a lot of Julia's powers come from its type system, it may be useful to have something such as macros—code that generates code—at a point where the compiler has inferred the types of the variables and function arguments in the program. Generated functions (also sometimes called *staged* functions) fulfill this need.

Using generated functions

Declaring a generated function is simple. Instead of the usual `function` keyword, generated functions are declared with the appropriately named `@generated function` keyword. This declares a function that can be called normally from any point in the rest of the program.

Generated functions come in two parts, which are related to how they are executed. They are invoked once for each unique type of its arguments. At this point, the arguments themselves take the values of their types. The return value of this execution must be an expression that is used as the body of the function when called with values of these types. This cycle is executed each time the function is called with new types. The function is called with types as values once, and then the returned expression is used for all invocations with argument values of this type.

More on generated functions

In this section, we quickly described how to write generated functions. We will not go into too much detail. For more information along with examples, please refer to the online Julia documentation

Using generated functions for performance

As with macros, strategies to use generated functions for performance revolve around moving constant parts of the computation earlier into the compilation stage. However, unlike macros, here the computations are fixed only for a certain type of argument. For different types of argument, the computations are different. Staged functions handle this difference elegantly.

As an example, let's consider a rather trivial problem: calculating the number of cells of a multidimensional array. The answer is of course a product of the number of elements in each dimension. As Julia has true multidimensional arrays, the number of dimensions, and the number of multiplications are not known upfront. One possible implementation is to loop over the number of dimensions, multiplying as we go:

```
function prod_dim{T, N}(x::Array{T, N})
    s = 1
    for i = 1:N
        s = s * size(x, i)
    end
    return s
end
```

Type parameters

Please review the Julia documentation on type parameters or refer to *Type parameters* section in *Chapter 3, Types in Julia*, if the preceding code looks unfamiliar.

This function will now work for arrays with any number of dimensions. Let's test this to see whether it works:

```
julia> prod_dim(rand(10,5,5))
250
```

Optimizing this computation with a generated function starts with the observation that the number of iterations of the loop is equal to the number of dimensions of the array, which is encoded as a type parameter for arrays. In other words, for a particular type of input (and array of a particular dimension), the loop size is fixed. So, what we can try to do in a generated function is move the loop to the compile time:

```
@generated function prod_dim_gen_impl{T, N}(x::Array{T, N})
    ex = :(1)
    for i = 1:N
        ex = :(size(x, $i) * $ex)
    end
    return ex
end
```

In this generated function, the loop runs at compile time when the type of x is known. We create an ex expression, which then becomes the body of the function when actually called with an instance of an array. We can see that this function works; it returns the same result as our earlier version with the loop:

```
julia>prod_dim_gen_impl(rand(10, 5,5))
250
```

However, it would be instructive to see the code that is generated and actually run for this function. For this purpose, we can paste the body of the generated function into a normal function, as follows:

```
function prod_dim_gen_impl{T, N}(x::Array{T, N})
    ex = :(1)
    for i = 1:N
        ex = :(size(x, $i) * $ex)
    end
    return ex
end
```

We can then call this function with the type of the arguments as input, and the returned expression will show us how this generated function works:

```
julia> x = rand(2, 2, 2);
julia> prod_dim_gen_impl(x)
:(size(x,3) * (size(x,2) * (size(x,1) * 1)))

julia> x = rand(2, 2, 2, 2);
julia> prod_dim_gen_impl(x)
:(size(x,4) * (size(x,3) * (size(x,2) * (size(x,1) * 1))))
```

It should be apparent what has happened here. For an array of three dimensions, we are multiplying three numbers; while for an array of four dimensions, we are multiplying two numbers. The loop of 1:N ran at compile time and then disappeared. The resulting code will be much faster without the loop, particularly if this function is called excessively in some other inner loop.

The technique of removing loops and replacing them with the calculations inline is usually called *loop-unrolling*, and it is often performed manually in performance-sensitive code. However, in Julia, generated functions are an easy and elegant way to achieve this without too much effort.

Also, note that this function looks much simpler without the loop. The number of tokens in this function is significantly reduced. This might make the function inline-worthy and cause the compiler to inline this function, making this code even faster.

Using named parameters

Julia supports a convenient named parameter syntax that is useful when creating complicated API with many optional parameters. However, the compiler cannot infer the types of named parameters effectively. Therefore, it should now be apparent that using named parameters can cause degraded performance.

As an example, we shall write the same function, once with named arguments, and once with regular, positional arguments. It will be apparent that the version with named arguments does not perform very well. (As an aside, note that the Benchmarks package that we've been using does not support named arguments. Therefore, we are benchmarking this code in a very simple way):

```
julia> named_param(x; y=1, z=1)  =  x^y + x^z
named_param (generic function with 1 method)


julia> pos_param(x,y,z) = x^y + x^z
pos_param (generic function with 1 method)


julia> @time for i in 1:100000;named_param(4; y=2, z=3);end
  0.032424 seconds (100.23 k allocations: 9.167 MB)


julia> @time for i in 1:100000;pos_param(4, 2, 3);end
  0.000832 seconds
```

It is apparent that using named parameters incurs a significant overhead in Julia. However, when designing high-level functions, it is still advantageous to use named parameters in order to create easy to use API's. Just don't use them in performance-sensitive inner loops.

Summary

In this chapter, we saw different ways to structure our code to make it perform better. The function is the primary element in Julia code; however, sometimes it is not the best option. Macros and generated functions can play an important role where appropriate.

In the next chapter, we will look deeper into the problem of numbers. We will see how Julia designs its core number types, and how to make basic numeric operations fly.

5
Fast Numbers

As it is a numerical programming language, fast computations with numbers are central to everything we do in Julia. In the previous chapters, we discussed how the Julia compiler and runtime perform across a wide range of code. In this chapter, we will take a detailed look at how these core constructs are designed and implemented in Julia.

In this chapter, we will cover the following topics:

- Numbers in Julia
- Trading performance for accuracy
- Subnormal numbers

Numbers in Julia

The basic number types in Julia are designed to closely follow the hardware on which it runs. The default numeric types are as close to the metal as possible—a design decision that contributes to Julia's C-like speed.

Integers

Integers in Julia are stored as binary values. Their default size, as in C, depends on the size of the CPU/OS on which Julia runs. On a 32-bit OS, the integers are 32 bits by default, and on a 64-bit machine, they are 64 bits by default. These two integer sizes are represented as different types within Julia: `Int32` and `Int64`, respectively. The `Int` type alias represents the actual integer type used by the system. The `WORD_SIZE` constant contains the bit width of the current Julia environment, which is as follows:

```
julia> WORD_SIZE
64
```

The `bits` function displays the underlying binary representation of the numbers. On a 64-bit machine, we get:

```
julia> bits(3)
"0000000000000000000000000000000000000000000000000000000000000011"
```

The default integer types are signed. That is, the first (and the most significant) bit is set to 1 to denote negative numbers, which are then stored as two's complement, as follows:

```
julia> bits(-3)
"1111111111111111111111111111111111111111111111111111111111111101"
```

Types such as these, and the following floating point types whose representation is simply a set of bits, have optimized handling within the Julia runtime. They are called *bits* types, and this feature can be queried for any type using the `isbits` function, as follows:

```
julia> isbits(Int64)
true

julia> isbits(ASCIIString)
false
```

One point to note is that, as a Julia value, basic numeric types can be boxed. That is, when stored in memory they are prefixed with a tag that represents their type. However, the Julia compiler is usually very good at removing any unnecessary boxing/unboxing operations. They can usually be compiled out. For example, we can define a function that adds two numbers and inspect the machine code that is generated and executed when this function is called via the following code:

```
myadd(x, y) = x + y
```

Looking at the output of of the following compiled code, (even if, like me, you are not an expert at reading assembly), it should be apparent that, other than the function overhead to set the stack and return the result, the generated code simply consists of the CPU instruction to add two machine integers, `addq`. There is no boxing/unboxing operation remaining in the native code when the function is called. Take a look at the following:

```
julia> @code_native myadd(1,2)
    .section  __TEXT,__text,regular,pure_instructions
Filename: none
Source line: 1
    pushq  %rbp
    movq   %rsp, %rbp
Source line: 1
    addq   %rsi, %rdi
    movq   %rdi, %rax
    popq   %rbp
    ret
```

There is an even bigger advantage to storing numbers using the machine representation. Arrays of these numbers can be stored using contiguous storage. A type tag is stored once at the start. Beyond this, data in numerical arrays is stored in a packed form. This not only means that these arrays can be passed to C libraries as-is (minus the type tag) but also that the compiler can optimize computations on these arrays easily. There is no need for pointer dereferencing when operating on numerical arrays of bit types.

Integer overflow

A further consequence of the decision to use machine integers by default is that there are no overflow checks present within any base mathematical operation in Julia.

With a fixed number of bytes available to represent integers of a certain type, the possible values are bounded. These bounds can be viewed using the typemax and typemin functions, as follows:

```
julia> typemax(Int64)
9223372036854775807

julia> bits(typemax(Int64))
"0111111111111111111111111111111111111111111111111111111111111111"

Julia> typemin(Int64)
-9223372036854775808

julia> bits(typemin(Int64))
"1000000000000000000000000000000000000000000000000000000000000000"
```

When the result of any operation is beyond the possible values for a type, it overflows. This typically results in the number being wrapped around from the maximum to the minimum, as in the following code:

```
julia> 9223372036854775806 + 1

9223372036854775807


julia> 9223372036854775806 + 1 + 1

-9223372036854775808


julia> typemin(Int64)

-9223372036854775808
```

Another way to think about an overflow is that, to represent larger numbers, additional bits are required in the most significant positions. These bits are then chopped off, and the remaining bits are returned as the result. Thinking about it this way explains many counterintuitive results when it comes to overflows. Take a look at the following code:

```
julia> 2^64

0

julia> 2^65

0
```

This behavior is very different from what is observed in popular dynamic languages, such as Ruby and Python. In these languages, every basic mathematical operation includes an overflow check. When the overflow is detected, the value is automatically upgraded to a wider type capable of storing the larger value. However, this causes a significant overhead to all numerical computation. Not only do we have to pay the cost for the extra CPU operation for the overflow check, but the conditional statement also prevents CPU pipelining from being effective. For this reason, Julia (as with Java and C) chooses to operate directly on machine integers and forgo all overflow checks.

This may be confusing and frustrating at first glance if you have a background in programming Python or Ruby, but this is the price you pay for high-performance computing. Once you understand that Julia's numbers are really close to the metal and designed to be directly operated on by the CPU, it should not be any more difficult to construct correctly behaving programs in practice.

BigInt

If you know your program needs to operate on large integers beyond the range of `Int32` or `Int64`, there are various options in Julia. First, if your numbers can still be bounded, there is `Int128`. However, for arbitrarily large integers, Julia has built-in support via the `BigInt` type. Run the following code:

```
julia> big(9223372036854775806) + 1 + 1
9223372036854775808


julia> big(2)^64
18446744073709551616
```

Operations on `Int128` are slower, and for `BigInts` they are much slower than for the default integers. However, we can use these in situations where they are warranted without compromising on the performance of computations that fit within the bounds of the default types.

The floating point

The default floating-point type is always 64-bits wide and is called `Float64`. This is true irrespective of the underlying machine and OS bit width. It is represented in memory using the IEEE 754 binary standard.

The IEEE 754 standard is the universally accepted technical standard for floating point operations in computer hardware and software. Almost all commonly used CPU types implement their floating-point support using this standard. As a result, storing numbers in this format means that the CPU (or rather the FPU — the floating point unit within the CPU) can operate on them natively and quickly.

The binary storage standard for 64-bit floating point numbers consists of 1 sign bit, 11 bits of exponent, and 52 bits of the mantissa (or the significand), as follows:

```
julia> bits(2.5)
"0100000000000100000000000000000000000000000000000000000000000000"


julia> bits(-2.5)
"1100000000000100000000000000000000000000000000000000000000000000"
```

Unchecked conversions for unsigned integers

The basic integers described previously are all signed values. Unsigned integers can be specified using the `UInt64` and `UInt32` types. As with many other Julia types, the type conversions can be done via type constructors, as follows:

```
julia> UInt64(UInt32(1))
0x0000000000000001
```

These conversions check for out-of-range values. They throw an error when trying to convert a value that does not fit in the resulting type, as follows:

```
julia> UInt32(UInt64(1))
0x00000001


julia> UInt32(typemax(UInt64))
ERROR: InexactError()
in call at essentials.jl:56
```

The conditional check will have an overhead when performing this calculation, not only because of following out the CPU's instructions but also due to pipeline failures. In some situations, when working with binary data, it may be acceptable to truncate 64-bit values to 32-bit values without checking. In such situations, there is a shortcut in Julia, which is to use the `%` operator with the type, as in the following code:

```
julia> typemax(UInt64) % UInt32
0xffffffff
```

Using this construct prevents any errors from being thrown for out-of-bound values, and it is much faster than the checked version of the conversion. This also works for other base unsigned types, such as `UInt16` and `UInt8`.

Trading performance for accuracy

In this book, we largely focus on performance. However, at this stage, it should be said that accurate math is usually an even bigger concern. All basic floating-point arithmetic in Julia follows strict IEEE 754 semantics. Rounding is handled carefully in all base library code to guarantee the theoretical best error limits. In some situations, however, it is possible to trade off performance for accuracy and vice versa.

The fastmath macro

The @fastmath macro is a tool to loosen the constraints of IEEE floating point operations in order to achieve greater performance. It can rearrange the order of evaluation to something with is mathematically equivalent but that would not be the same for discrete floating point numbers due to rounding/error effects. It can also replace some intrinsic operations with their faster variants that do not check for NaN or Infinity. This results in faster operation but might cause a compromise in accuracy. This option is similar to the -ffast-math compiler option in clang or GCC.

As an example, consider the following code that calculates the finite difference between the elements of an array and then sums them. We can create two versions of the function that are identical except for the fact that one has the @fastmath annotation and one doesn't. Simply use the following code:

```
function sum_diff(x)
    n = length(x); d = 1/(n-1)
    s = zero(eltype(x))
    s = s +  (x[2] - x[1]) / d
    for i = 2:length(x)-1
        s =  s + (x[i+1] - x[i+1]) / (2*d)
    end
    s = s + (x[n] - x[n-1])/d
end

function sum_diff_fast(x)
    n=length(x); d = 1/(n-1)
    s = zero(eltype(x))
    @fastmath s = s +  (x[2] - x[1]) / d
    @fastmath for i = 2:n-1
        s =  s + (x[i+1] - x[i+1]) / (2*d)
    end
    @fastmath s = s + (x[n] - x[n-1])/d
end
```

We can note that the @fastmath macro can be used in front of statements or loops. In fact, it can be used in front of any block of code, including functions. Anything relevant within this block will be rewritten by the macro.

Benchmarking the two implementations shows that @fastmath provides an approximate *2.5x* improvement over the base version. Take a look at the following:

```
julia> t=rand(2000);

julia> sum_diff(t)
46.636190420898515

julia> sum_diff_fast(t)
46.636190420898515

julia> @benchmark sum_diff(t)
================= Benchmark Results ========================
      Time per evaluation: 5.74 µs [5.68 µs, 5.81 µs]
Proportion of time in GC: 0.00% [0.00%, 0.00%]
        Memory allocated: 0.00 bytes
    Number of allocations: 0 allocations
        Number of samples: 3901
    Number of evaluations: 82201
          R² of OLS model: 0.987
 Time spent benchmarking: 0.53 s


julia> @benchmark sum_diff_fast(t)
================= Benchmark Results ========================
      Time per evaluation: 2.10 µs [2.09 µs, 2.11 µs]
Proportion of time in GC: 0.00% [0.00%, 0.00%]
        Memory allocated: 0.00 bytes
    Number of allocations: 0 allocations
        Number of samples: 4901
    Number of evaluations: 213901
          R² of OLS model: 0.997
 Time spent benchmarking: 0.50 s
```

This result is very much dependent on the nature of the computation. In many situations, the improvements are much lower. Also, in this case, the two functions return the exact same value, which is not true in the general case. The message, then, is to test and measure extensively when using this feature.

As with everything else in Julia, we can introspect and take a look at what changes the macro makes to our code. We can observe that the macro rewrites the intrinsic functions with its own _fast versions in the following code:

```julia
julia> macroexpand(:(@fastmath for i=2:n-1; s =  s + (x[i+1] -
x[i+1]) / (2*d); end))

:(for i = 2:Base.FastMath.sub_fast(n,1) # none, line 1:
        s =
Base.FastMath.add_fast(s,Base.FastMath.div_fast(Base.FastMath.sub_fas
t(x[Base.FastMath.add_fast(i,1)],x[Base.FastMath.add_fast(i,1)]),Base
.FastMath.mul_fast(2,d)))
    end)
```

The K-B-N summation

Adding a collection of floating point values is a very common operation, but it is surprisingly susceptible to the accumulation of errors. A naïve implementation—that is, adding elements from the first to the last—accumulates errors at the rate of $O(\sqrt{n})$, where n is the number of elements being summed. Julia's sum base uses a pairwise summation algorithm that does better by accumulating errors at $O\left(\sqrt{\log(n)}\right)$ but is almost as fast. However, there exists a more complicated summation algorithm attributed to William Kahan whose error is bound by $O(1)$. This is implemented in Julia in the sum_kbn function.

In order to test the accuracy of sum, we will use a set of numbers that are particularly susceptible to rounding errors. The sum of the set of three numbers (1, -1, and 10^{-100}) should be 10^{-100}. However, as one of these numbers is much smaller than the other two, the result will be incorrectly rounded to 0. Take a look at the following code:

```julia
julia> sum([1 1e-100 -1])

0.0


julia> sum_kbn([1 1e-100 -1])

1.0e-100


julia> @benchmark sum([1 1e-100 -1])

================ Benchmark Results ========================
      Time per evaluation: 6.72 ns [6.68 ns, 6.75 ns]
 Proportion of time in GC: 0.00% [0.00%, 0.00%]
         Memory allocated: 0.00 bytes
     Number of allocations: 0 allocations
```

```
        Number of samples: 10701
    Number of evaluations: 53712201
        R² of OLS model: 0.991
  Time spent benchmarking: 0.52 s


julia> @benchmark sum_kbn([1 1e-100 -1])
================ Benchmark Results ========================
      Time per evaluation: 9.53 ns [9.47 ns, 9.60 ns]
Proportion of time in GC: 0.00% [0.00%, 0.00%]
        Memory allocated: 0.00 bytes
    Number of allocations: 0 allocations
        Number of samples: 10601
    Number of evaluations: 48829501
        R² of OLS model: 0.987
  Time spent benchmarking: 0.52 s
```

In summary, the default sum function is adequate for most situations. It is fast and quite accurate. However, for pathological cases or when summing millions of elements, the sum_kbn function may give up some performance in favor of increased accuracy.

Subnormal numbers

Subnormal numbers (also sometimes called denormal) are very small floating point values near zero. Formally, they are numbers *smaller* than those that can be represented without leading zeros in the significand (for example, normal numbers). Typically, floating point numbers are represented without leading zeros in the significand. Leading zeros in the number are moved to the exponent (that is, *0.0123* is represented as *1.23x10⁻²*). Subnormal numbers are, therefore, numbers in which such a representation would cause the exponent to be lower than the minimum possible value. In such a situation, the significand is forced to have leading zeros. Much more detail on these numbers is available on Wikipedia at https://en.wikipedia.org/wiki/Denormal_number.

Subnormal numbers in Julia can be identified by the issubnormal function, as follows:

```
julia> issubnormal(1.0)
false


julia> issubnormal(1.0e-308)
true
```

Subnormal numbers are useful for a gradual underflow. Without them, for example, subtraction between extremely small values of floating point numbers might underflow to zero, causing subsequent *divide-by-zero* errors. This is shown in the following code:

```julia
julia> 3e-308 - 3.001e-308
-1.0e-311

julia> issubnormal(3e-308 - 3.001e-308)
true
```

Subnormal numbers to zero

Subnormal numbers cause a significant slowdown on modern CPUs, sometimes by up to *100x*. This may be hard to track down because these performance problems can occur when the inputs take certain values even if we hold the algorithm constant. They manifest as unexplained, intermittent slowdowns.

One solution would be to force all subnormal numbers to be treated as zero. This will set a CPU flag that discards all the subnormal numbers and uses zero in its place. While this solves the performance problem, it should be used with care as it may cause accuracy and numerical stability problems. In particular, it is no longer true that $x-y == 0 => x == y$, as can be noted in the following code:

```julia
julia> set_zero_subnormals(true)
true

julia> 3e-308 - 3.001e-308
-0.0

julia> 3e-308 == 3.001e-308
false

julia> get_zero_subnormals()
true
```

One of the ways subnormal numbers arise is when a calculation exponentially decays to zero. This gradual flattening of the curve results in many subnormal numbers being created and causes a sudden performance drop. As an example, we will take a look at one such computation here:

```
function timestep( b, a, dt )
    n = length(b)
    b[1] = 1
    two = eltype(b)(2)
    for i=2:n-1
        b[i] = a[i] + (a[i-1] - two*a[i] + a[i+1]) * dt
    end
    b[n] = 0
end

function heatflow( a, nstep )
    b = similar(a)
    o = eltype(a)(0.1)
    for t=1:div(nstep,2)
        timestep(b,a,o)
        timestep(a,b,o)
    end
end
```

We will then benchmark these functions with and without forcing subnormal numbers to zero. We can note a speedup by around two times by forcing subnormal numbers to zero. Take a look at the following:

```
julia> set_zero_subnormals(false)
true


julia> @benchmark heatflow(a, 1000)
================= Benchmark Results ========================
      Time per evaluation: 4.19 ms [2.29 ms, 6.09 ms]
Proportion of time in GC: 0.00% [0.00%, 0.00%]
        Memory allocated: 3.98 kb
   Number of allocations: 1 allocations
       Number of samples: 100
   Number of evaluations: 100
 Time spent benchmarking: 0.46 s
```

```
julia> set_zero_subnormals(true)
true


julia> @benchmark heatflow(a, 1000)
================= Benchmark Results ========================
     Time per evaluation: 2.20 ms [2.06 ms, 2.34 ms]
Proportion of time in GC: 0.00% [0.00%, 0.00%]
        Memory allocated: 3.98 kb
   Number of allocations: 1 allocations
       Number of samples: 100
   Number of evaluations: 100
 Time spent benchmarking: 0.25 s
```

Summary

In this chapter, we discussed how Julia uses a machine representation of numbers to achieve C-like performance for its arithmetic computations. We noted how to work within these design constraints and considered the edge cases that are introduced.

Working with single numbers, however, is the easy part. Most numerical computations, as we noted throughout this book, consist of working on large sets of numbers. In the next chapter, we will take a look at how to make arrays perform fast.

6
Fast Arrays

It should not be a surprise to readers of this book that array operations are often the cornerstone of scientific and numeric programming. While arrays are a fundamental data structure in all programming, there are special considerations when they are used in numerical programming. One particular difference is that arrays are not just viewed as entities for data storage. Rather, they represent the fundamental mathematical structures of vectors and matrices.

In this chapter, we will discuss how to use arrays in Julia in the fastest possible way. When you profile your program, you will find that, in many cases, the majority of its execution time is spent in array operations. Therefore, the discussions in this chapter will likely turn out to be crucial in creating high-performance Julia code. The following are the topics we will cover:

- Array internals and storage
- Bounds checks
- In-place operations
- Subarrays
- SIMD parallelization
- Yeppp! for fast vector operations
- Writing generic library functions using arrays

Array internals in Julia

We discussed how Julia's performance comes out of using *type* information to compile specific and fast machine code for different data types. Nowhere is this more apparent than in array-related code. This is probably where all of Julia's design choices pay off in creating high-performance code.

Array representation and storage

An array type in Julia is parameterized by the type of its elements and the number of its dimensions. Hence, the type of an array is represented as `Array{T, N}`, where `T` is the type of its elements, and `N` is the number of dimensions. So, for example, `Array{UTF8String, 1}` is a one-dimensional array of strings, while `Array{Float64,2}` is a two-dimensional array of floating point numbers.

Type parameters

You must have realized that type parameters in Julia do not always have to be other types; they can be constant values as well. This makes Julia's type system enormously powerful. It allows the type system to represent complex relationships and enables many operations to be moved to compile (or dispatch) time rather than at runtime.

Representing the type of an element within the type of arrays as a type parameter allows powerful optimization. It allows arrays of primitive types (and many immutable types) to be stored inline. In other words, the elements of the array are stored within the array's own primary memory allocation.

In the following diagram, we will show this storage mechanism. The numbers in the top row represent array indexes, while the numbers in the boxes are the integer elements stored within the array. The numbers in the bottom row represent the memory addresses where each of these elements is stored:

	[1]	[2]	[3]	[4]	[5]	[6]
Values	15	22	32	56	34	55
	1000	1004	1008	1012	1016	1020

In most other dynamic languages, all arrays are stored using pointers to their values. This is usually because the language runtime does not have enough information about the types of values to be stored in an array and hence cannot allocate the correctly sized storage. As represented in the following figures, when an array is allocated, contiguous storage simply consists of pointers to the actual elements, even when these elements are primitive types that can be stored natively in memory.

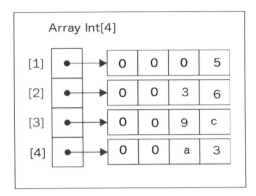

This method of storing arrays inline, without pointer indirection as much as possible, has many advantages and, as we discussed earlier, is responsible for much of Julia's performance claims. In other dynamic languages, the type of every element of the array is uncertain and the compiler has to insert type checks on each access. This can quickly add up and become a major performance drain.

Further, even when every element of the array is of the same type, we pay the price of memory load for every array element if they are stored as pointers. Given the relative costs of a CPU operation versus a memory load on a modern processor, not doing this is a huge benefit.

There are other benefits too. When the compiler and CPU notice operations on a contiguous block of memory, CPU pipelining and caching are much more efficient. Some CPU optimizations, such as **Single Instruction Multiple Data (SIMD)**, are also unavailable when using indirect array loads.

Column-wise storage

When an array has only one dimension, its elements can be stored one after the other in a contiguous block of memory. As we observed in the previous section, operating on this array sequentially from its starting index to its end can be very fast, being amenable to many compiler and CPU optimizations.

Two-dimensional or higher arrays can, however, be stored in two different ways. We can store them row-wise or column-wise. In other words, we can store from the beginning of the array the elements of the first row, followed by the elements of the second row, and so on. Alternatively, we can store the elements of the first column, then the elements of the second column, and so on.

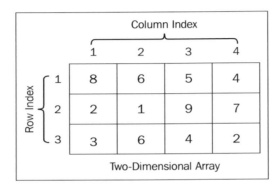

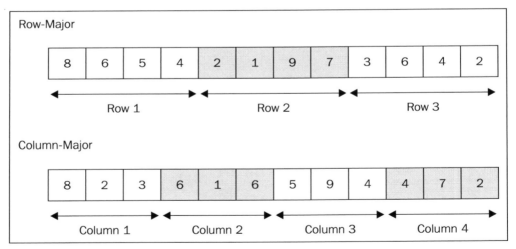

Arrays in C are stored as row-ordered. Julia, on the other hand, chooses the latter strategy, storing arrays as column-ordered, similar to MATLAB and Fortran. This rule applies to higher-dimensional arrays as well. In Julia, the array is stored with the last dimension first.

Naming convention

Conventionally, the term *row* refers to the first dimension of a two-dimensional array, and *column* refers to the second dimension. As an example, for a two-dimensional array of x::Array{Float64, 2} floats, the expression x[2,4] refers to the elements in the second row and the fourth column.

This particular strategy of storing arrays has implications for how we navigate them. The most efficient way to read an array is in the same order in which it is laid out in memory. That is, each sequential read should access contiguous areas in memory.

We can demonstrate the performance impact of reading arrays in sequence with the following code, which squares and sums the elements of a two-dimensional floating point array, writing the result at each step back to the same position. This code exercises both the read and write operations for the array:

```julia
function col_iter(x)
    s=zero(eltype(x))
    for i = 1:size(x, 2)
        for j = 1:size(x, 1)
            s = s + x[j, i] ^ 2
            x[j, i] = s
        end
    end
end

function row_iter(x)
    s=zero(eltype(x))
    for i = 1:size(x, 1)
        for j = 1:size(x, 2)
            s = s + x[i, j] ^ 2
            x[i, j] = s
        end
    end
end
```

The `row_iter` function operates on the array in the first order row, while the `col_iter` function operates on the array in the first order column. We expect, based on the description of the previous array storage, that the `col_iter` function would be considerably faster than the `row_iter` function. Running the benchmarks, this is indeed what we see, as follows:

```
julia> a = rand(1000, 1000);


julia> @benchmark col_iter(a)
================ Benchmark Results ========================
    Time per evaluation: 2.37 ms [1.64 ms, 3.10 ms]
Proportion of time in GC: 0.00% [0.00%, 0.00%]
        Memory allocated: 0.00 bytes
   Number of allocations: 0 allocations
        Number of samples: 100
   Number of evaluations: 100
 Time spent benchmarking: 0.28 s


julia> @benchmark row_iter(a)
================ Benchmark Results ========================
    Time per evaluation: 6.53 ms [4.99 ms, 8.08 ms]
Proportion of time in GC: 0.00% [0.00%, 0.00%]
        Memory allocated: 0.00 bytes
   Number of allocations: 0 allocations
        Number of samples: 100
   Number of evaluations: 100
 Time spent benchmarking: 0.71 s
```

The difference between the two is quite significant. Column major access is more than twice as fast. This kind of difference in the inner loop of an algorithm can make a very noticeable difference in the overall runtime. It is, therefore, crucial to consider the order in which multidimensional arrays are processed when writing performance-sensitive code.

Bound checking

Like most dynamic languages, the Julia runtime performs bound checks on arrays by default. This means that the Julia compiler and runtime verify that the arrays are not indexed outside their limits and that all the indexes lie between the actual start and end of an array. Reading values of memory mistakenly beyond the end of an array is often the cause of many bugs and security issues in unmanaged software. Hence, bound checking is an important determinant of safety in your programs.

Removing the cost of bound checking

However, as with any extra operation, bound checking has costs too. There are extra operations for all array reads and writes. While this cost is reasonably small and is usually a good trade-off for safety, in some situations, where it can be guaranteed that the array bounds are never crossed, it may be worthwhile to remove these checks. This is possible in Julia using the `@inbounds` macro, as follows:

```
function prefix_bounds(a, b)
    for i = 2:size(a, 1)
        a[i] = b[i-1] + b[i]
    end
end

function prefix_inbounds(a, b)
    @inbounds for i = 2:size(a, 1)
        a[i] = b[i-1] + b[i]
    end
end
```

The `@inbounds` macro can be applied in front of a function or loop definition. Once this is done, all bound checking is disabled within the code block annotated with this macro. The performance benefit of doing this is small but may be significant overall for hot inner loops. Take a look at the following code:

```
julia> @benchmark prefix_bounds(x, y)
================ Benchmark Results ========================
    Time per evaluation: 1.78 ms [1.72 ms, 1.83 ms]
Proportion of time in GC: 0.00% [0.00%, 0.00%]
      Memory allocated: 0.00 bytes
   Number of allocations: 0 allocations
      Number of samples: 100
  Number of evaluations: 100
Time spent benchmarking: 0.20 s
```

```
julia> @benchmark prefix_inbounds(x, y)
================ Benchmark Results ========================
        Time per evaluation: 1.50 ms [1.24 ms, 1.76 ms]
Proportion of time in GC: 0.00% [0.00%, 0.00%]
        Memory allocated: 0.00 bytes
    Number of allocations: 0 allocations
        Number of samples: 100
    Number of evaluations: 100
 Time spent benchmarking: 0.17 s
```

The `@inbounds` annotation should only be used when it can be guaranteed that the array access within the annotated block will never be out of bounds. This typically should be only when the limits of the loop depend directly on the length of the array — that is, for code of the `for i in 1:length(array)` form. If the programmer disables bound checking for some code and the array access is actually out of bounds, the results will be undefined. At best, the program will crash quickly.

Configuring bound checks at startup

The Julia runtime can use a command-line flag to set up bound-checking behavior for the entire session. The `-check-bounds` option can take two values: `yes` and `no`. These options will override any macro annotation in the source code.

When the Julia environment is started with `-check-bounds=yes`, all `@inbounds` annotations in code are ignored, and bound checks are mandatorily performed. This option is useful when running tests to ensure that code errors are properly reported and debugged if any.

Alternatively, when the Julia runtime is started with `-check-bounds=no`, no bound checking is done at all. This is equivalent to annotating all array access with the `@inbounds` macro. This option should only be used sparingly in the case of extremely performance-sensitive code, in which the system is very well tested and with minimal user inputs.

Allocations and in-place operations

Consider the following trivial function, xpow, which takes an integer as input and returns the first few powers of the number. Another function, xpow_loop, uses the first function to compute the sum of squares of a large sequence of numbers, as follows:

```
function xpow(x)
    return [x x^2 x^3 x^4]
end

function xpow_loop(n)
    s = 0
    for i = 1:n
      s = s + xpow(i)[2]
    end
    return s
end
```

Benchmarking this function for a large input shows that this function is quite slow, as follows:

```
julia> @benchmark xpow_loop(1000000)
================ Benchmark Results ========================
     Time per evaluation: 103.17 ms [101.39 ms, 104.95 ms]
Proportion of time in GC: 13.15% [12.76%, 13.53%]
       Memory allocated: 152.58 mb
   Number of allocations: 4999441 allocations
       Number of samples: 97
   Number of evaluations: 97
 Time spent benchmarking: 10.16 s
```

The clue is in the number of allocations displayed in the preceding output. Within the xpow function, a four-element array is allocated for each invocation of this function. This allocation and the subsequent garbage collection take a significant amount of time. The Proportion of time in GC statistic displayed in the preceding code snippet also hints at this problem.

Preallocating function output

Note that, in the xpow_loop function, we only require one array at a time to compute our result. The array returned from one xpow call is differenced in the next iteration of the loop. This suggests that all these allocations for new array are a waste, and it may be easier to preallocate a single array to hold the result for each iteration, as follows:

```
function xpow!(result::Array{Int, 1}, x)
    @assert length(result) == 4
    result[1] = x
    result[2] = x^2
    result[3] = x^3
    result[4] = x^4
end

function xpow_loop_noalloc(n)
    r = [0, 0, 0, 0]
    s = 0
    for i = 1:n
        xpow!(r, i)
        s = s + r[2]
    end
    s
end
```

Note that the xpow! function now has an exclamation mark in its name. This Julia convention denotes that this function takes an output variable that mutates as an argument. We allocate a single variable outside the loop in the xpow_loop_noalloc function and then use it in all loop iterations to store the result of the xpow! function. Take a look at the following code:

```
@benchmark xpow_loop_noalloc(1000000)

================= Benchmark Results =========================
    Time per evaluation: 11.02 ms [10.47 ms, 11.57 ms]
Proportion of time in GC: 0.00% [0.00%, 0.00%]
       Memory allocated: 96.00 bytes
   Number of allocations: 1 allocations
      Number of samples: 100
  Number of evaluations: 100
 Time spent benchmarking: 1.13 s
```

The result of this change is quite impressive. The runtime of the function, doing the same computation, decreases by an order of magnitude. Even more impressively, instead of millions of allocations, the program got by with only a single allocation.

The message, then, is simple: pay attention to what allocations happen within your inner loops. Julia provides you with simple tools to track this, so this is easy to fix. In fact, we don't need a full-fledged benchmarking infrastructure to figure this out. The simple @time macro also displays the allocations clearly, as shown by the following code:

```
julia> @time xpow_loop(1000000)
  0.115578 seconds (5.00 M allocations: 152.583 MB, 21.99% gc time)


julia> @time xpow_loop_noalloc(1000000)
  0.011720 seconds (5 allocations: 256 bytes)
```

Mutating versions

Given what we discussed in the previous section about the benefits of preallocating output, it should come as no surprise that many base library functions in Julia have mutating counterparts that modify their arguments rather than allocating a new output structure.

For example, the sort base library function, which sorts an array, allocates a new array of the same size as its input to hold its output: the sorted array. On the other hand, sort! makes an in-place sorting operation, in which the input array is itself sorted, as follows:

```
Julia> @benchmark sort!(a)
================ Benchmark Results =========================
        Time per evaluation: 15.92 ms [15.16 ms, 16.69 ms]
  Proportion of time in GC: 0.00% [0.00%, 0.00%]
          Memory allocated: 0.00 bytes
    Number of allocations: 0 allocations
        Number of samples: 100
    Number of evaluations: 100
  Time spent benchmarking: 1.63 s
```

```
julia> @benchmark sort(a)
================ Benchmark Results ========================
      Time per evaluation: 18.51 ms [17.22 ms, 19.80 ms]
 Proportion of time in GC: 4.78% [0.34%, 9.22%]
        Memory allocated: 7.63 mb
   Number of allocations: 4 allocations
       Number of samples: 100
   Number of evaluations: 100
 Time spent benchmarking: 1.90 s
```

In this case, while the performance difference is significant, note that the allocating version of the function spends a significant proportion of its time in garbage collection and allocates a large amount of memory.

Array views

Julia, similarly to most scientific languages, has a very convenient syntax for array slicing. Consider the following example that sums each column of a two-dimensional matrix. First, we will define a function that sums the elements of a vector to produce a scalar. We will then use this function inside a loop to sum the columns of a matrix, passing each column one by one to our vector adder, as follows:

```
function sum_vector(x::Array{Float64, 1})
    s = 0.0
    for i = 1:length(x)
        s = s + x[i]
    end
    return s
end

function sum_cols_matrix(x::Array{Float64, 2})
    num_cols = size(x, 2)
    s = zeros(num_cols)
    for i = 1:num_cols
        s[i] = sum_vector(x[:, i])
    end
    return s
end
```

The x[:, j] syntax denotes all the row elements of the jth column. In other words, it slices a matrix into its individual columns. Benchmarking this function, we will notice that the allocations and GC times are quite high. Take a look:

```
julia> @benchmark sum_cols_matrix(rand(1000, 1000))
================ Benchmark Results ========================
      Time per evaluation: 4.45 ms [3.45 ms, 5.46 ms]
Proportion of time in GC: 17.55% [3.19%, 31.91%]
        Memory allocated: 7.76 mb
   Number of allocations: 3979 allocations
      Number of samples: 100
  Number of evaluations: 100
 Time spent benchmarking: 0.48 s
```

The reason for the high allocation is the fact that in Julia, array slices create a copy of the slice. In other words, for every x[:, j] slice operation in the preceding code snippet, a new vector is allocated to hold the column, and the element values are copied into it from the original matrix. This obviously causes a large overheard in this kind of algorithms.

What we would like in this case is to create a vector representing one column of the matrix that shares its storage with the original array. This saves a significant amount of allocation and copying.

Julia 0.4 includes a sub() function, which does exactly this. It returns a new array that is actually a view into the original array. Creating a SubArray is very fast, much faster than creating a sliced copy. Accessing a SubArray can be slower than accessing a regular dense array, but Julia's standard library has some extremely well-tuned code for this purpose. This code achieves performance nearly on a par with using regular arrays.

Using sub(), we can rewrite our sum_cols_matrix function to reduce the allocations due to slicing. However, first, we need to loosen the parameter type of sum_vector, as we will now pass SubArray to this function. The SubArray type is a subtype of AbstractArray, but it is obviously a different type than the Array concrete type, which denotes dense, contiguous stored arrays. Take a look at the following code:

```
function sum_vector(x::AbstractArray)
    s = 0.0
    for i = 1:length(x)
        s = s + x[i]
    end
```

```
        return s
    end


function sum_cols_matrix_views(x::Array{Float64, 2})
    num_cols = size(x, 2); num_rows = size(x, 1)
    s = zeros(num_cols)
    for i = 1:num_cols
        s[i] = sum_vector(sub(x, 1:num_rows, i))
    end
    return s
end
```

We can note that this function, which uses the views of arrays to operate on portions of them, is significantly faster than using slices and copies. Most importantly, in the following benchmark, the number of allocations and the time spent in GC are much lower, as follows:

```
julia> @benchmark sum_cols_matrix_views(rand(1000, 1000))
================ Benchmark Results ========================
    Time per evaluation: 1.38 ms [1.06 ms, 1.71 ms]
Proportion of time in GC: 0.81% [0.00%, 5.64%]
        Memory allocated: 101.64 kb
   Number of allocations: 3001 allocations
       Number of samples: 100
   Number of evaluations: 100
 Time spent benchmarking: 0.18 s
```

SIMD parallelization

SIMD is the method of parallelizing computation whereby a single operation is performed on many data elements simultaneously. Modern CPU architectures contain instruction sets that can do this, operating on many variables at once.

Say you want to add two vectors, placing the result in a third vector. Let's imagine that there is no standard library function to achieve this, and you were writing a naïve implementation of this operation. Execute the following code:

```
function sum_vectors!(x, y, z)
    n = length(x)
    for i = 1:n
        x[i] = y[i] + z[i]
    end
end
```

Say the input arrays to this function has 1,000 elements. Then, the function essentially performs 1,000 sequential additions. A typical SIMD-enabled processor, however, can add maybe eight numbers in one CPU cycle. Adding each of the elements sequentially can, therefore, be a waste of CPU capabilities.

On the other hand, rewriting code to operate on parts of the array in parallel can get complex quickly. Doing this for a wide range of algorithms can be an impossible task. Julia, as you would expect, makes this significantly easier using the @simd macro. Placing this macro against a loop gives the compiler the freedom to use SIMD instructions for the operations within this loop if possible, as shown in the following code:

```
function sum_vectors_simd!(x, y, z)
    n = length(x)
    @inbounds @simd for i = 1:n
        x[i] = y[i] + z[i]
    end
end
```

With this one change to the function, we can now achieve significant performance gains on this operation, as follows:

```
julia> @benchmark sum_vectors!(zeros(Float32, 1000000), rand(Float32, 1000000), rand(Float32, 1000000))
================ Benchmark Results ========================
    Time per evaluation: 1.88 ms [1.73 ms, 2.03 ms]
Proportion of time in GC: 0.00% [0.00%, 0.00%]
      Memory allocated: 0.00 bytes
  Number of allocations: 0 allocations
     Number of samples: 100
  Number of evaluations: 100
Time spent benchmarking: 0.24 s


julia> @benchmark sum_vectors_simd!(zeros(Float32, 1000000), rand(Float32, 1000000), rand(Float32, 1000000))
================ Benchmark Results ========================
    Time per evaluation: 1.02 ms [980.93 µs, 1.06 ms]
Proportion of time in GC: 0.00% [0.00%, 0.00%]
      Memory allocated: 0.00 bytes
  Number of allocations: 0 allocations
```

```
      Number of samples: 100
   Number of evaluations: 100
 Time spent benchmarking: 0.24 s
```

There are a few limitations to using the @simd macro. This does not make every loop faster. In particular, note that using SIMD implies that the order of operations within and across the loop might change. The compiler needs to be certain that the reordering will be safe before it attempts to parallelize a loop. Therefore, before adding @simd annotation to your code, you need to ensure that the loop has the following properties:

- All iterations of the loop are independent of each other. That is, no iteration of the loop uses a value from a previous iteration or waits for its completion. The significant exception to this rule is that certain reductions are permitted.
- The arrays being operated upon within the loop do not overlap in memory.
- The loop body is straight-line code without branches or function calls.
- The number of iterations of the loop is obvious. In practical terms, this means that the loop should typically be expressed on the length of the arrays within it.
- The subscript (or index variable) within the loop changes by one for each iteration. In other words, the subscript is unit stride.
- Bounds checking is disabled for SIMD loops. (Bound checking can cause branches due to exceptional conditions.)

To check whether the compiler successfully vectorized your code, use the @code_llvm macro to inspect the generated LLVM bitcode. While the output might be long and inscrutable, the keywords to look for in the output are sections prefixed with vector and vectorized operations that look similar to <n * float>.

The following is an extract from the output of @code_llvm for the function we ran before, showing a successful vectorization of the operations. Thus, we know that the performance gains we observed are indeed coming from an automatic vectorization of our sequential code:

```
julia> @code_llvm sum_vectors_simd!(zeros(Float32, 1000000),
rand(Float32, 1000000), rand(Float32, 1000000))

.........


vector.ph:                                             ; preds = %if3
  %n.vec = sub i64 %20, %n.mod.vf
  %28 = sub i64 %n.mod.vf, %20
```

```
br label %vector.body


vector.body:                                        ; preds =
%vector.body, %vector.ph
  %lsr.iv42 = phi i64 [ %lsr.iv.next43, %vector.body ], [ 0,
  %vector.ph ]
  %29 = mul i64 %lsr.iv42, -4
  %uglygep71 = getelementptr i8* %25, i64 %29
  %uglygep7172 = bitcast i8* %uglygep71 to <8 x float>*
  %wide.load = load <8 x float>* %uglygep7172, align 4
  %30 = mul i64 %lsr.iv42, -4
  %sunkaddr = ptrtoint i8* %25 to i64
  %sunkaddr73 = add i64 %sunkaddr, %30
  %sunkaddr74 = add i64 %sunkaddr73, 32
  %sunkaddr75 = inttoptr i64 %sunkaddr74 to <8 x float>*
  %wide.load14 = load <8 x float>* %sunkaddr75, align 4
```

Yeppp!

Many algorithms for scientific computing compute transcendental functions (log, sin, and cos) on arrays of floating point values. These are heavily used operations with strict correctness requirements and thus have been the target of many optimization efforts over the years. Faster versions of these functions can have a huge impact on the performance of many applications in the scientific computing domain.

In this area, the **Yeppp!** software suite can be considered state-of-the-art. Primarily written at Georgia Institute of Technology by Marat Dukhan, Yeppp! provides optimized implementations of modern processors of these functions, which are much faster compared to the implementations in system libraries.

Julia has a very easy-to-use binding to Yeppp! within a package. It can be installed using the in-built package management mechanism `Pkg.add("Yeppp")`. Once installed, the functions are available with the `Yeppp` module. There is no simpler way to get a *4x* performance boost. With performance gains of this magnitude, there is little reason to use anything else for code where a large number of transcendental functions needs to be computed. Run the following code:

```
julia> @benchmark log(a)
================ Benchmark Results ========================
```

```
      Time per evaluation: 17.41 ms [16.27 ms, 18.55 ms]
 Proportion of time in GC: 5.08% [0.32%, 9.83%]
        Memory allocated: 7.63 mb
   Number of allocations: 2 allocations
        Number of samples: 100
    Number of evaluations: 100
 Time spent benchmarking: 1.81 s
```

```
julia> @benchmark Yeppp.log(a)
================ Benchmark Results ========================
      Time per evaluation: 4.45 ms [3.54 ms, 5.35 ms]
 Proportion of time in GC: 15.63% [1.55%, 29.71%]
        Memory allocated: 7.63 mb
   Number of allocations: 2 allocations
        Number of samples: 100
    Number of evaluations: 100
 Time spent benchmarking: 0.49 s
```

Yeppp also provides in-place versions of its functions that can be faster in many situations, saving allocations and subsequent garbage collection. The in-place version of log, for example, provides a *2x* performance gain over the allocating version we ran before. Take a look at the following code:

```
julia> @benchmark Yeppp.log!(a)
================ Benchmark Results ========================
      Time per evaluation: 2.34 ms [2.01 ms, 2.67 ms]
 Proportion of time in GC: 0.00% [0.00%, 0.00%]
        Memory allocated: 0.00 bytes
   Number of allocations: 0 allocations
        Number of samples: 100
    Number of evaluations: 100
 Time spent benchmarking: 0.26 s
```

The Yeppp Julia package provides implementations of some common vectorized functions, including log, sin, exp, and sumabs. Refer to https://github.com/JuliaLang/Yeppp.jl for full details of its capabilities.

Writing generic library functions with arrays

The suggestions in the previous sections should make your array code fast and high-performance. If you are directly writing code to solve your own problems, this should be enough. However, if you are writing library routines that may be called by other programs, you will need to heed additional concerns. Your function may be called with arrays of different kinds and with different dimensions. To write generic code that is fast with all types and dimensions of arrays, your code needs to be careful in how it iterates over the elements of the arrays.

All Julia arrays are subtypes of the `AbstractArray` type. All abstract arrays must provide facilities for indexation and iteration. However, these can be implemented very differently for different types of arrays. The default array is `DenseArray`, which stores its elements in contiguous memory. As discussed before, these elements can be pointers or values, but in either case, they are stored in contiguous memory. This means that linear indexing is very fast for all these arrays. However, this is not true for all kinds of arrays.

Linear indexing

The term *linear indexing* refers to the ability of indexing a multidimensional array by a single scalar index. So, for example, if we have a three-dimensional array x with 10 elements in each dimension, it can be indexed with a single integer in the range of 1 to 1000. In other words, $x[1]$, $x[2]$,…$x[10]$, $x[11]$, …$x[99]$, and $x[100]$ are consecutive elements of the array. As described earlier, Julia arrays are stored in a major order column, so linear indexing runs through the array in this order. This makes linear indexing particularly cache-friendly because contiguous memory segments are accessed consecutively. In contrast, *cartesian indexing* uses the complete dimensions of the array to index it. The three-dimensional array x is indexed by three integers $x[i, j, k]$.

For example, subarrays can be efficiently indexed using cartesian indexing, but linear indexing is much slower due to the need to compute a div for each indexing operation. While cartesian indexing is useful when the dimensions of an array are known, generic code typically uses linear indexing to work with multidimensional arrays. This, then, may create performance pitfalls.

As an example of a function that can work with generic multidimensional arrays, let's write a simple function that sums all the elements in an array, as follows:

```
function mysum_linear(a::AbstractArray)
    s=zero(eltype(a))
    for i = 1:length(a)
        s=s+a[i]
    end
    return s
end
```

This function works with arrays of any type and dimension, as we can note in the test calls in the following code, in which we call it with a range—a three-dimensional array, a two-dimensional array, and a two-dimensional subarray, respectively:

```
julia> mysum_linear(1:1000000)
500000500000

julia> mysum_linear(reshape(1:1000000, 100, 100, 100))
500000500000

julia> mysum_linear(reshape(1:1000000, 1000, 1000))
500000500000

julia> mysum_linear(sub(reshape(1:1000000, 1000, 1000), 1:500, 1:500) )
62437625000
```

If we benchmark these functions, we will note that calling the same function on a subarray is significantly slower than calling it on a regular dense array.

```
julia> @benchmark mysum_linear(reshape(1:1000000, 1000, 1000))
================ Benchmark Results ========================
      Time per evaluation: 808.98 µs [728.67 µs, 889.28 µs]
Proportion of time in GC: 0.00% [0.00%, 0.00%]
        Memory allocated: 0.00 bytes
   Number of allocations: 0 allocations
       Number of samples: 100
   Number of evaluations: 100
 Time spent benchmarking: 0.33 s
```

```
julia> @benchmark mysum_linear(sub(reshape(1:1000000, 1000, 1000), 1:500,
1:500) )

================ Benchmark Results ========================
      Time per evaluation: 11.39 ms [10.23 ms, 12.55 ms]
Proportion of time in GC: 4.97% [0.75%, 9.19%]
        Memory allocated: 7.61 mb
   Number of allocations: 498989 allocations
        Number of samples: 100
   Number of evaluations: 100
  Time spent benchmarking: 1.34 s
```

In situations such as this where we want to write generic functions that can be performant with different kinds of arrays, the advice is to not use linear indexing. So, what should we use?

The simplest option is to directly iterate the array rather than iterating its indices. The iterator for each kind of array will choose the most optimal strategy for high performance. Hence, the code to add the elements of a multidimensional array can be written as follows:

```
function mysum_in(a::AbstractArray)
    s = zero(eltype(a))
    for i in a
        s = s + i
    end
end
```

If we benchmark this function, we can see the difference in performance, as follows:

```
julia> @benchmark mysum_in(sub(reshape(1:1000000, 1000, 1000), 1:500,
1:500) )

================ Benchmark Results ========================
      Time per evaluation: 354.25 µs [347.11 µs, 361.39 µs]
Proportion of time in GC: 0.00% [0.00%, 0.00%]
        Memory allocated: 0.00 bytes
   Number of allocations: 0 allocations
        Number of samples: 100
   Number of evaluations: 100
  Time spent benchmarking: 0.23 s
```

This strategy is usable when the algorithm only requires the elements of the array and not its indexes. If the indexes need to be available within the loop, they can be written using the `eachindex()` method. Each array defines an optimized `eachindex()` method that allows the iteration of its index efficient. We can then rewrite the sum function as follows, even though, for this particular function, we do not actually need indexes:

```
function mysum_eachindex(a::AbstractArray)
    s = zero(eltype(a))
    for i in eachindex(a)
        s = s + a[i]
    end
end
```

The benchmark numbers demonstrate an order of magnitude improvement in the speed of these functions when not using linear indexing for subarrays. Writing code in this manner, therefore, allows our function to be used correctly and efficiently by all manner of arrays in Julia. Take a look at the following:

```
Julia> @benchmark mysum_eachindex(sub(reshape(1:1000000, 1000, 1000),
1:500, 1:500) )

================ Benchmark Results ========================
      Time per evaluation: 383.06 µs [363.04 µs, 403.07 µs]
Proportion of time in GC: 0.00% [0.00%, 0.00%]
        Memory allocated: 0.00 bytes
   Number of allocations: 0 allocations
       Number of samples: 100
   Number of evaluations: 100
 Time spent benchmarking: 0.22 s
```

Summary

In this chapter, we covered the performance characteristics in Julia of the most important data structure in scientific computing: the array. We discussed why Julia's design enables extremely fast array operations and how to get the best performance in our code when operating on arrays. This brings us to the end of our journey creating the fastest possible code in the Julia. Using all the tips discussed until now, the performance of your code should approach that of well-written C.

Sometimes, however, this isn't enough; we want higher performance. Our data may be larger or our computations intensive. In this case, the only option is to parallelize our processing using multiple CPUs and systems. In the next chapter, we will take a brief look at the features that Julia provides to write parallel systems easily.

Beyond the Single Processor

7

Throughout this book, we discussed ways to make our code run faster and more efficiently. Using the suggestions in the previous chapters, your code now fully utilizes the processor without much overhead or wastage. However, if you still need your computation to finish even earlier, the only solution is distributing the computation over multiple cores, processors, and machines. In this chapter, we will briefly discuss some of the facilities available in Julia for distributed computing. A complete exposition of this topic is probably the subject of another large book—this chapter can only provide a few pointers for further information, such as:

- Parallelism in Julia
- Programming parallel tasks
- Shared memory arrays

Parallelism in Julia

Julia is currently a single-threaded language (although it does perform asynchronous I/O). This means that the Julia code that you write will run sequentially on a single core of the machine. There are a few significant exceptions; Julia has asynchronous I/O that can offload network or file access to a separate operating system thread, and some libraries embedded within Julia, such as OpenBLAS, spawn and manage multiple threads for their computations. Notwithstanding these exceptions, most user-written Julia code is limited to a single core.

Julia, however, contains an easy-to-use multiprocessor mechanism. You can start multiple Julia processes either on a single host or across a network, and you can control, communicate, and execute programs across the entire cluster.

Starting a cluster

The communication between Julia processes is *one-sided* in the sense of there being a master process that accepts the user's inputs and controls all the other processes. Starting a cluster, therefore, involves either a command-line switch while starting the master Julia process or calling methods from REPL. At its simplest, the -p n option while starting Julia creates *n* additional processes on the local host, as can be seen in the following:

```
$ ./julia -p 2


    _          _ _(_)_          |  A fresh approach to technical computing
   (_)        | (_) (_)         |  Documentation: http://docs.julialang.org
    _ _   _| |_  __ _           |  Type "?help" for help.
   | | | | | | | |/ _` |        |
   | | |_| | | | | (_| |        |  Version 0.4.3-pre+6 (2015-12-11 00:38 UTC)
  _/ |\__'_|_|_|\__'_|          |  Commit adffe19* (63 days old release-0.4)
 |__/                           |  x86_64-apple-darwin15.2.0
```

The procs() method can be used to inspect the cluster. It returns the IDs of all the Julia processes that are available. We can note in the following that we have three processes available—the master and two child processes:

```
julia> procs()
3-element Array{Int64,1}:
 1
 2
 3
```

The addprocs(n) method creates additional processes connected to the same master. It behaves similarly to the -p n option but is a pure Julia function that can be called from REPL or other Julia code, as follows:

```
julia> addprocs(2)
2-element Array{Int64,1}:
 4
 5


julia> procs()
```

```
5-element Array{Int64,1}:
 1
 2
 3
 4
 5
```

These commands launch multiple Julia processes on the same machine. This is useful to the extent of running as many Julia processes as the number of cores on this host. Beyond this, you can start processes on other hosts by providing the hostname to the addprocs call, as follows:

```
julia> addprocs(["10.0.2.1", "10.0.2.2"])
```

```
7-element Array{Int64,1}:
 1
 2
 3
 4
 5
 6
 7
```

This invocation, by default, uses **Secure Shell (SSH)** to connect to and start Julia processes on remote machines. There are, of course, many different configuration options possible for this setup, including the ability to use other protocols to control and communicate between processes. All this and more is described in detail in the manual at http://docs.julialang.org/en/release-0.4/manual/parallel-computing/#clustermanagers.

Communication between Julia processes

The primitive facilities provided by Julia to move code and data within a cluster of processes consist of *remote references* and *remote calls*. As the name suggests, a remote reference consists of a reference to data residing on a different Julia process. Thereby, values can be retrieved from (or written to) such a reference.

A remote call, on the other hand, is a request to execute a function on a particular node. Such a call is asynchronous in that a remote calls finishes immediately, returning the RemoteRef object, which is a reference to its result. The arguments to remotecall are the function name, the process number to execute the function in, and the arguments to this function. The caller, then, has the option to wait() on the reference until the call completes and then fetch() the result into its own process, as shown in the following code:

```julia
julia> a = remotecall(2,sqrt, 4.0)
RemoteRef{Channel{Any}}(2,1,3)

julia> wait(a)
RemoteRef{Channel{Any}}(2,1,3)

julia> fetch(a)
2.0
```

For simple uses, the remotecall_fetch function can combine these two steps and return the function result at once, as follows:

```julia
julia> remotecall_fetch(2, sqrt, 4.0)
2.0
```

Programming parallel tasks

The low-level facilities that we saw in the previous section are quite flexible and very powerful. However, they leave a lot to be desired in terms of ease of use. Julia, therefore, has built-in set of higher-level programming tools that make it much easier to write parallel code. We will discuss some of them in the next section.

@everywhere

The @everywhere macro is used to run the same code in all the processes in the cluster. This is useful to set up the environment to run the actual parallel computation later. The following code loads the Distributions package and calls the rand method on all the nodes simultaneously, as follows:

```julia
julia> @everywhere using Distributions

julia> @everywhere rand(Normal())
```

@spawn

The @spawn macro is a simpler way to run a function in a remote process without having to specify the remote node or having to work through ambiguous syntax. Take a look at the following code:

```julia
julia> a=@spawn randn(5,5)^2
RemoteRef{Channel{Any}}(2,1,240)


julia> fetch(a)
5x5 Array{Float64,2}:
 -0.478348  -0.185402    6.21775    2.62166   -5.4774
 -3.22569   -1.56487     3.03402   -0.305334  -1.75827
 -2.9194    -0.0549954   0.922262  -0.117073  -0.281402
  0.709968   1.87017    -1.7031     0.343585   0.09105
  3.20311    0.49899    -0.202174  -0.337815  -1.81711
```

This macro actually creates a closure around the code being called on the remote node. This means that any variable declared on the current node will be copied over to the remote node. In the preceding code, the random array is created on the remote node. However, in the following code, the random array is created on the current node and copied to the remote node. Even though the two code extracts look similar, they have very different performance characteristics. Take a look at the following code:

```julia
julia> b=rand(5,5)
5x5 Array{Float64,2}:
 0.409983  0.852665   0.490156  0.481329  0.642901
 0.676688  0.0865577  0.59649   0.553313  0.950665
 0.591476  0.824942   0.440399  0.701106  0.321909
 0.137929  0.0138369  0.273889  0.677865  0.33638
 0.249115  0.710354   0.972105  0.617701  0.969487


julia> a=@spawn b^2
RemoteRef{Channel{Any}}(3,1,242)


julia> fetch(a)
5x5 Array{Float64,2}:
 1.26154  1.29108  1.68222  1.73618  2.01716
 1.00195  1.75952  1.7217   1.7541   1.81713
```

1.2381	1.17741	1.48089	1.72401	1.8542
0.405205	0.593076	0.709137	0.933354	0.744132
1.48451	1.77305	2.08556	2.21207	2.29608

Parallel for

Julia includes an inbuilt **parallel for** loop that can automatically distribute the computation within a for loop across all the nodes in a cluster. This can sometimes allow code to be sped up across machines with little programmer intervention.

In the following code, we will generate a million random numbers and add them. The first function computes each step serially, while the second function attempts to distribute the steps across the cluster. Each step in this loop can be computed independently and should thus be easy to parallelize:

```
function serial_add()
    s=0.0
    for i = 1:1000000
       s=s+randn()
    end
    return s
end
```

```
function parallel_add()
    return @parallel (+) for i=1:1000000
        randn()
    end
end
```

We can note that the parallel function provides a significant performance improvement without the programmer having to manage the task distribution or internode communication explicitly. Now, take a look at the following code:

```
julia> @benchmark serial_add()
================ Benchmark Results ========================
    Time per evaluation: 6.95 ms [6.59 ms, 7.31 ms]
Proportion of time in GC: 0.00% [0.00%, 0.00%]
        Memory allocated: 0.00 bytes
   Number of allocations: 0 allocations
        Number of samples: 100
   Number of evaluations: 100
 Time spent benchmarking: 0.86 s
julia> @benchmark parallel_add()
```

```
================ Benchmark Results ========================
      Time per evaluation: 4.42 ms [4.25 ms, 4.60 ms]
Proportion of time in GC: 0.00% [0.00%, 0.00%]
        Memory allocated: 154.42 kb
   Number of allocations: 2012 allocations
       Number of samples: 100
   Number of evaluations: 100
  Time spent benchmarking: 0.63 s
```

Parallel map

The parallel for loop we discussed in the previous section can perform a reduction (the addition in the previous code) and works well even if each step in the computation is lightweight. For code where each iteration is heavyweight, and there is no reduction to be done, the parallel map construct is useful. In the following code, we will create 10 large matrices and then perform a singular-value decomposition on each. We can note that parallelizing this computation can attain a significant speed improvement simply by changing one character in the code:

```
julia> x=[rand(100,100) for i in 1:10];

julia> @benchmark map(svd, x)
================ Benchmark Results ========================
      Time per evaluation: 327.77 ms [320.38 ms, 335.16 ms]
Proportion of time in GC: 0.13% [0.00%, 0.40%]
        Memory allocated: 5.47 mb
   Number of allocations: 231 allocations
       Number of samples: 29
   Number of evaluations: 29
  Time spent benchmarking: 10.18 s
julia> @benchmark pmap(svd, x)
================ Benchmark Results ========================
      Time per evaluation: 165.30 ms [161.76 ms, 168.84 ms]
Proportion of time in GC: 0.10% [0.00%, 0.40%]
        Memory allocated: 1.66 mb
   Number of allocations: 2106 allocations
       Number of samples: 59
   Number of evaluations: 59
  Time spent benchmarking: 10.11 s
```

Distributed arrays

The DistributedArrays package provides an implementation of partitioned multidimensional arrays. Detailed package documentation is available at https://github.com/JuliaParallel/DistributedArrays.jl. For the moment, it suffices to say that there exist facilities to partition datasets automatically at creation or manually, as well as distributing the computation to each node for operation on the local parts of the arrays.

Shared arrays

Distributed arrays are a fully generic solution that scales across many networked hosts in order to work on data that cannot fit in the memory of a single machine. However, in many circumstances, although the data does fit in the memory, we want multiple Julia processes to improve throughput by fully utilizing all the cores in a machine. In this situation, shared arrays are useful to get different Julia processes operating on the same data.

Shared arrays, as the name suggests, are arrays that are shared across multiple Julia processes on the *same* machine.

Constructing SharedArray requires specifying its type, its dimensions, and the list of process IDs that will have access to the array, as follows:

```
S=SharedArray( Float64, (100, 100, 5), pids=[2,3,4,5]);
```

Once a shared array is created, it is accessible in full to all the specified workers (on the same machine). Unlike a distributed array, the data is not partitioned, and hence there is no need for any data transfer between nodes. Therefore, when the data is small enough to fit in the memory but large enough to require multiple nodes to process, shared arrays are particularly useful. Not only are they highly performant in these situations, it is much easier to write code for them.

Threading

Shared arrays can be seen as some kind of shared memory multiprocessing in Julia. They are currently useful as Julia does not have first-class threads that can operate on shared memory. This is, however, being worked on as we speak, and it is likely that in the future versions of Julia, it will be possible to operate on shared memory arrays from multiple threads within the same process.

Summary

This chapter provided a very cursory glimpse into the parallel computing facilities built into the Julia language. While we didn't cover much in detail in this chapter, you have hopefully noted how easy it is to get started with distributed computation in Julia. With a little bit of help from the online documentation, it should be easy to create high performing distributed codebases in Julia.

Index

Symbols

A

B

C

D

F

G